Feeling My Way

Also by Gerry Tamm

Choosing Life: A Diary of Grace
Making Sense: An Elder's Task

Contributor

Variations on the Ordinary: A Woman's Reader

Editor

Heart Songs
Anthology of the Poetry Society of Michigan, 1995
Mingled Threads
Anthology of AAUW, Dearborn Writers Group

Feeling My Way

A Journey To Self-Discovery

Gerry Tamm

ISBN: 978-1547292837

For my fellow travelers and guides on this journey.

My thanks to family and friends who listened to my stories and to my writing groups who guided the progress of my writing. A special thank you to Tom Ziegler for the cover photo and to Evalyn Bennet-Alder who helped edit the manuscript.

Contents

Birth

I gave birth to myself when I was well into my middle years. This is how it happened.

On a glorious spring morning fifteen retreatants gathered in the comfortably furnished main lounge of St. Basil's Conference Center, a former monastery perched on a hill north of Detroit. A wall of windows in that sunlit room overlooked a valley of greening trees spread like patchwork under a blue sky untouched by city smog.

Our leader Doug directed each of us to find a space in the room where we could spread out on the floor undisturbed and cover ourselves completely with one of the blankets provided for us. The task was to return to the womb by curling up under our blankets. I found my corner, unfolded my blanket, took a deep breath, and wrapped up. Claustrophobic as I am, I dreaded covering my face. My chest constricted as I began to breathe my own exhalations. I felt like I was suffocating.

You can do this, I told myself. *For fifteen minutes you can do this.*

I curled myself into the fetal position and waited. Soon the apprehension faded. The warmth felt good. My breathing slowed and deepened. I gradually relaxed and melted into the cocoon surrounding me. At first I was flooded with sexual feelings. My boundaries expanded and my body flowed in waves. I uncurled, luxuriating like a cat stretching out of a nap in the sun. Suddenly I felt an overwhelming anger, followed by sheer panic. I felt trapped. I had to get out. I struggled against the smothering blanket tangled about my limbs. Finally I threw it aside and took a deep breath, my heart pounding. I was born. After my escape from that angry womb, I relaxed into the certain knowledge that in the bedroom where I was born I had been placed in the welcoming arms of my grandmother.

I have no doubt that I recaptured fetal memories etched into my developing body that day. The stories of my birth explain the feelings that had washed through me during the exercise. I was born at home to a rebellious mother who would not stay in the hospital to give birth. She kicked up such a fuss that Dr. Moore and my grandmother agreed to return her to her own bed for the event.

Tantrums were not out of character for my mother. She dropped out of high school when she was sixteen because of an altercation with her home economics teacher. She refused to eat an egg she had cooked. Lord knows what she did with it but clearly she did not quietly slip it into a wastebasket or her purse. Suspended from the class until she apologized to the teacher, she quit school rather than bend.

And that was not her first act of rebellion. She refused to answer at her mother's divorce hearing, when the judge asked her about her father's violence. She was his favorite of the five children, the youngest of the four girls. She loved him and would not betray him. Loyal or spoiled? Or simply stubborn? She told me this story with a great deal of pride in what she had done. After all he had never laid a finger on her, she said.

She blamed her mother for her unhappiness. Scornfully she said her mother had left behind a big wonderful house in Cleveland for the cramped quarters of a fancy suburban address on Grace Avenue in Lakewood, the house where I was born.

It was a white frame, two-family flat, two bedrooms, one

2

bath, a living room, dining room, kitchen, and a front porch on each floor, typical of houses of the twenties and thirties. I find it hard to believe that it was a fancy address. It makes more sense that a divorced woman with five children would need the income from the upper flat and could make do with limited space until the kids were on their own.

Mother clings to her resentment like the child she was when it all happened. She had lost her pampering father and had to live with the woman she considered responsible for the loss.

I suspect that mother's marriage was another act of rebellion. My father came from a family with money. My early childhood memories include images of the dark, polished wood of the broad staircase in the foyer of what seemed to be a mansion to me. There was an impressive fireplace in the parlor. Huge wood sliding doors could be closed to separate the parlor from a dining room and the spacious sunny kitchen as big as half our house. I remember having tea in that kitchen with my grandmother Bennett. She put a lemon drop in my china cup because she had no lemon. I was no more than four years old at the time.

My father came from a rather disreputable family. My grandfather, a retired river boat captain, was a bookie. Mother sometimes answered the phone and took bets for him when he was away. One day she took a large bet on a longshot from my grandfather's good friend who was with him at the racetrack that day. It was too close to post time to lay off part of the bet and the horse won. The outcome is somewhat murky but it did end my grandfather's career.

Mother admired my regal, silver-haired grandmother, a real lady, she said. But when she spoke of my grandfather, her disapproving words were belied by the unconcealed admiration in her voice for his rakish charm. I suspect that he was a replacement for her own father, banished from her life by my grandmother.

My father must have had some of his father's dash. Certainly his flirtation with the scandalous appealed to her own disrespect for authority. It was the twenties, the era of prohibition and flappers. Mother must have loved the times and the man who introduced her to a glamorous world.

They were married four years before I made my appearance. She was again living in the unhappy home of her teens, forced to share her bedroom with the boarders my grandmother had taken in. All the glamour of her life had evaporated a week before my birth when she received a phone call from a friend congratulating her on her new baby boy. But there I was, still confined to her womb.

It seems that another Bennett baby was listed in the birth notices, son of Raymond and coincidentally Helen, my mother's name. Yes, it was my father's child. No wonder I felt that anger in the womb, that blissful place suddenly turned alien. No wonder my grandmother gave in to her demands and brought her home to her girlhood bed, away from the hospital where my half-brother was born a week earlier. No wonder she looked at her redheaded baby with distaste.

I thank God for my grandmother who took me into her arms and her heart and gave me five years of her devotion.

Living on Grace

God is warm. God is safe. God is cozy. God is a circle of light cast by the bedside lamp enclosing my grandmother and me in her shadowed room. God is in my grandmother's voice as she reads His word to me in Slovak.

Every night Gramma sits next to my bed in her nightshirt. She loosens the knot of her long grey hair and slowly brushes it. Then she reads aloud from the Bible. After this nightly ritual she climbs into bed with me and we sleep under the billowy featherbed--the *parina*.

During the day I have my own sunny corner of the dining room and Gramma is in the kitchen. We are separated by the wall between us but our voices reach back and forth to each other.

"What's Slovak for baby?" I am dressing my doll.

"What's Slovak for flower?" I am looking out the window.

"What's Slovak for tablecloth?" I am hiding under the table

When I picture that room, it is the lower half that I see, eye level about table height. This tells me that these are very early memories. I have stretched back as far as I can remember

A buffet fills one wall of the room. It is taller than the table and has three sections: cupboards at each end, two wide drawers between them. Four legs support each cupboard section with cross members on three sides making two cozy enclosures under the buffet. I use one of these spaces as a potty. When my mother discovers this, she scolds me but for some reason I think Gramma laughs.

On the adjacent wall at the opposite end of the room is a triple window with a dark wood window seat where Gramma keeps her plants. There are built-in cupboards underneath and on each side a drawer at surface level. Above that are cupboards with beveled glass doors for china. I have a drawer and a cupboard for my things in the corner where I play when Gramma is in the kitchen. A heat register between the dining room and the kitchen keeps my corner warm and cozy and the sun shining through the windows makes it bright.

There is a round table in the middle of the room with a massive pedestal and four carved feet that look like bear claws. I like to play under the table, sitting on the bear feet. When company comes, they gather around that table for coffee and cards, beer and conversation. When they play cards, I sit on Gramma's lap and help her play the kings and queens.

The chairs are high-backed with posts on each side of a panel with a convex curve on top, rising up in the middle as high as the posts. One day Gramma threw me across one of these chair backs-- the curve fit my body neatly--and spanked me. I can still feel the back of that chair cutting into my waist. That hurt more than the spanking. A glimmer of memory wonders if this was the time my mother told me about later. I had had convulsions and she dunked me in cold water. Perhaps Gramma had whacked me first because I was holding my breath.

We ate our dinner at that table every Sunday, chicken soup with homemade noodles, then chicken and vegetables in the soup plates. I remember lying awake in bed listening to the plop, plop, plop of noodles on the floured board where Gramma tossed them every Sunday morning before church.

One Sunday morning while she was at church, I was playing with my dolls in my corner and spilled talcum powder on the dark wood of the window seat. I rubbed it into the ledge and it clouded the wood. I sprinkled more and rubbed it in so that it matched the rest. More and more. Somehow it got on the plants. When Gramma got home she had a fit. But she wasn't angry at me. She was angry at my mother who was sleeping instead of watching me. Mother worked nights and slept late mornings. I took care of myself.

I told this story in a Re-evaluation Counseling session where my partner mimicked my circular rubbing motion and encouraged me to tell the story over and over again. I laughed uncontrollably as I relived my amazement at the powder whitening the wood, spreading it farther and farther with my rubbing. Tears streamed down my face as I laughed. Telling and retelling clarified the details and the feelings of the experience. It loosened other memories of the time that I had blocked out of my memory and I felt again the love and security of my grandmother's care.

Gramma takes me to God's house on the corner where I go to Sunday School while she attends services. Gramma teaches me to cross the street, swinging my head back and forth in both directions looking for what I don't know, there are so few cars in the neighborhood.

Gramma takes me to ballet lessons. I don't want to go. I whine and complain about the tight shoes. She took me every week until my recital then refused to put up with the fuss any more. That was the end of ballet lessons.

Then Gramma disappeared. My memories stop. When I tell my writers group about this, they are alarmed when I say that when I was five Gramma dropped off the face of the earth. I quickly explain , "Well, she moved to New Jersey."

"Same thing," they say and we all laugh.

They tell me to write how I felt. I tell them I felt nothing. They can't believe me. If Gramma said goodbye, I can't remember. If anyone explained, I can't remember. I was numb.

It was not until I was in therapy some 40 years later that I thought to ask who it was that took Gramma away from me. Where had he come from? Mother told me he was a man Gramma had known in the old country. His wife had died and he wrote to her from New Jersey and asked her to come and marry him. That's why I had never seen him until I visited her there.

I do not remember when my Aunt Rose and Uncle Jim moved into the house on Grace. I do not remember when I moved out of Gramma's bed into the bedroom where I was born to share a bed with my mother. Sally and Belle, Gramma's boarders, were gone. My cousin Janice, seven years older, slept in a single bed across the room from the double bed where Mother and I slept. My mother continued to work nights and sleep days.

I looked forward to her days off when she promised to take me places. Time and time again she went off without me. I would walk with her to the streetcar on Madison Avenue, watch her get on and ride away. Then I walked home alone past the corner store, past the empty lots next to the church, then the church, around the corner past my friend Mary Ann's house, then Gramma's friend's house, then home. Without Gramma it was a lonely place.

The new minister of the church moved into the house next door, fourth from the corner. I played with his daughter Ruth and began Sunday School again. The first church service I attended was an evening Lenten service. I loved to sing and I counted the pages of print between the hymns in the hymnal.

One day I was walking along Madison Avenue--I was about seven--and saw a poster in a store window advertising Good Friday services. It was purple and black bordered in white. It was Jesus on the cross wearing the crown of thorns, bleeding, weeping, suffering--for me. Somehow I knew this. I felt the pain. From then on purple meant suffering.

When I moved away from Grace Avenue, I left God's house behind. Girl friends in my new neighborhood would take me to other churches but they did not seem the same. For me God's house will

8

always be Gothic, with stained glass and carved wood and marble, resounding organs, candles, huge trees at Christmas, lilies at Easter and purple in preparation for those days of rejoicing. God became the father I never had, the perfect father who loves me as I am, who never leaves me, even during those years on the brink of adulthood when I questioned the beliefs of my church.

Gramma welcomed me into the world and gave me the gift of God.

The Lady In Blue

When I was four years old, I wanted to go to school more than anything in the world. Mother promised that when I was five years old I could go, an impossible promise. I expected to go to school the day after my birthday. I begged and begged. I nagged my mother to call and see if I could come. We had no telephone at home, so she would take me to phone booths and make calls, talk to someone, then tell me that I couldn't go until September.

It was only April. After Gramma left, the days were endless. Mother took a new job at a magazine stand in the Terminal Tower in downtown Cleveland. She worked days so I saw very little of her.

We moved into an apartment. I have very few mental images of that time. I remember one day standing on the sidewalk near the front door of the building wearing a sweater and cap, nothing to do, no one to play with. Mother sent me outside and she wouldn't let me back in so I just stood and waited.

Another day I sat at the table with a poached egg on toast in front of me. I sat on my hands and swung my legs. I would not eat the egg. The runny yolk was yukky and the toast under it was soggy. Mother sat at the table next to me waiting for me to eat it while I stubbornly refused. I think she finally gave up. Perhaps she remembered the egg fiasco in Home Ec and took pity on me.

Our brief attempt at apartment living came to an end the night that I lay in the murphy bed and watched my baby sitter smooch with her boyfriend while Mother was out. I think I mentioned his name the next day and when she realized what was going on, that was the end of the sitter and the apartment. We returned to Grace to live with Aunt Rose, Uncle Jim, and my sixteen year old cousin Janice. Those years were difficult for me and they must have been terrible for Mother. She did not get along well with her sister, so I am sure she spent very little time at the house.

I finally started kindergarten at Franklin school, six blocks from our house. I loved my teacher Mrs. Brandt. She reminded me of my grandmother. My only complaint with school was the fat broken crayons we had to use. I couldn't do a decent job of drawing or coloring with those awful things and only seven colors besides. I wanted my 16 Crayolas with points and hoped for a set of 32 for Christmas. I was already adept at coloring complicated coloring books, drawing recognizable pictures, and printing a few words.

In the middle of the school year Mother and I moved again, this time to a room in the home of one of Mother's friends and her family. It was on the east side of Cleveland, foreign territory. I don't remember much about the house except that it had two stories for only one family. Houses were closer together and taller.

On the way to school we had to cross a bridge over train tracks that scared me. The friend's kids laughed at me but at least they stayed with me until I got used to the traffic, the trains, and the rumbling bridge. I caught chicken pox while I lived there and Mrs. Brandt came to visit me and brought me two jigsaw puzzles. Not the board puzzles that kids have today but real puzzles. One was Snow White. I loved them.

I don't know what occasioned our return to Grace this time but the next time my mother moved out, she left me behind. At least I was back in familiar territory with Aunt Rose, Uncle Jim, and my friends.

I spent most of my days outside. The house was at the top of a hill, an exciting place to coast on roller skates, scooters, bicycles, and sleds. When Gramma was there, my only friend was Mary Ann, two houses away, next door to the church. Now I went down the hill to Lou Ann's and across the street from her house to Johnny's and farther down the street to the corner of Franklin to Judy's. She had a play house in the back yard!

When I started kindergarten, my territory expanded to include the six blocks to Franklin school, usually down Grace and across Franklin, but sometimes across Madison and down the street the school was on. I also discovered the library. It was a block away but I had to walk two blocks out of the way so that I could cross busy Madison at the light. I remember disobeying that order one day thinking I was old enough to manage Madison traffic. But there was a gas station on the corner and cars coming and going that confused the issue. It was too scary. The cars were enormous and going in all directions. I was very small.

In the other direction on Madison were the stores. On Saturdays Mother gave me a dime to buy paper dolls at the dime store. Mary Ann and I shopped together to choose our books, then came back to cut them out in the basement of her house or ours. We had "graduated" to corners of our basements after having been forbidden to play with each other because of some childish spat or indiscretion which I can't remember. We were about six at the time. Neither of us was allowed in the house or yard of the other. The church steps on busy Madison Avenue became our sanctuary. We played there on the broad granite steps out of sight of our families. Eventually we were allowed to play under the huge pear tree next to the garage in our back yard, then finally we were assigned basement space.

At our house we had to pass the dreaded monster of a coal furnace and the gritty coal bin to get there. At her house there was a cozy storage space under the stairs that became ours. We spent hours cutting out and playing with paper dolls, the store-bought kind like the Ziegfield girls and those cut out of newspapers and magazines like Tillie the Toiler and Betsy McCall. I had a cardboard carton full of them that was reduced to a soggy mess during a rainstorm when the basement window was left open, one more tragedy in my young life. It ended my paper doll phase and I went on to comic books.

School and the library opened up undreamed of vistas for me. I devoured books and lived in make-believe worlds. I also developed new insights into adults. Mrs. Brandt knew children. Not so the librarian. I was probably seven when I asked her for a Christmas story. She gave me Dickens *Christmas Carol*. I took it home and read the words but could not make sense of it. After that I did not ask for her advice. I combed the shelves for myself until I found what I wanted. Librarians are still my last resort when researching. Independence came early and lasted long.

I grew up surprisingly trustful considering the mystifying behavior of the adults in my life: the unexplained disappearance of my grandmother, the brouhaha over Mary Ann and me, the irate Mr. MacGregor who chased us away when we turned somersaults on the tempting iron pipe fence that outlined his picture perfect lawn, the dishonesty of my Aunt Rose who, when I showed her five dollar bills that I had found on the sidewalk, as quick as a flash, deposited two of them in her apron pocket, handed the rest back to me and never suggested that we find the rightful owner.

Also there was my cousin Janice, a grown-up in my eyes, who did her share of taunting me. But that sometimes backfired.

Down the hill and across the street was a legendary neighborhood mansion we called the Widow's house. It was an imposing three-story, grey house. built on two lots, surrounded by trees and shrubs, a huge magnolia tree in the side yard. Picture the Addams' family mansion and you're close. There was never a sign of life around it. The neighborhood kids were all afraid of the spooky place but I didn't know that. Janice and her friends told me that I could

13

collect a lot of newspapers for the school paper drive if I went there. They stood aside giggling as I walked up the several wooden steps, across the wraparound veranda, too spacious to be called a porch, rang the bell, and waited at the massive door. It was stained wood framing an inset of leaded, beveled-glass, curtained with lace. The door opened to a world I had not seen since my Grandmother Bennett died. I could see the polished wood floor of the foyer, a mirror above a hall table, a carpeted stairway.

I gazed up at a tall, slender, silver-haired woman dressed in the most beautiful, floor length, blue silk gown that I had ever seen. She smiled down at me and waited for me to speak.

"Do you have any old newspapers?" I stammered. "We're having a paper drive at school."

"Yes, I do," she said, "but you will need something to carry them in. Do you have a wagon?"

"I have my doll buggy."

"Then come back tomorrow and I'll have the papers ready."

I returned the next day and had the last laugh on my cousin and her friends when I pushed home my wicker doll buggy piled high with bundles of old newspapers.

My friend Judy--with the play house in her back yard!--lived two doors down from the Widow's house and often visited her. One day I went along. The Widow led us up the staircase, its strip of richly patterned carpet softening our steps, to the ballroom on the third floor. She brought out a large wooden chest and placed it on the floor. She opened the lid to reveal a brass disc with pricky pins poking up all over it. Judy and I watched in fascination as she turned the crank on the side of the chest. Music spilled all around us. I was transfixed as I listened to the tinkling music.

I ran my fingers across the polished wood floor where we sat. It felt smooth and warm from the sun shining through the low uncurtained windows. I felt like I did in my corner of Gramma's house when I played in the dining room and talked to Gramma in the kitchen. I played in that corner when I was alone in the house but it had changed. It was dark and gloomy now and had a skin-crawling feel. My own place, where my things were, was down in the scary basement past the monster furnace I dreaded.

The Widow showed me a new, wonderful world. When I think of her, it is always in that marvelous blue, somewhere between cornflower and sapphire, still one of my favorite colors. Many years ago when my mother was widowed, I made her a silky caftan that color. I did not consciously think of the Widow when I chose the material, but I'm sure that my unconscious recognized it immediately.

I was giving my mother the graciousness and tranquillity that I had experienced at the Widow's house. Later I bought her a Marblehead Print tote bag in the same color. And when she had surgery at age 75, widowed for a second time, she could not stay warm even in the Florida sun. I knitted her a shoulder shawl in soft luxury yarn in mixed shades of that marvelous blue.

"It doesn't go with any of my clothes," she complained.

"It's not meant to be worn away from home, Mother. It's meant to keep you cozy watching TV or reading in bed."

When she died fifteen years later it was not among her things.

The Dream

I was nine years old when I finally moved away from the house where I was born into the home of Aunt Hazel, not a blood aunt but a close friend of my father's family. Soon after that I had a dream: I am dancing and singing in a ring of pretty little girls all dressed up in ruffly, pastel-colored party dresses. Below us somewhere a huge sooty man with a dark beard and black clothes–the coal man--presses the button on an elevator car and it begins its slow ascent toward us. I woke in a cold sweat. I had the dream at least twice more and I was so frightened by it that I dreaded sleep. Every night I prayed to my loving Father to take away that dream. The dream stopped but the fear triggered by the dream was locked into my body not to be released until a bitterly cold February night thirty-one years later.

Over the years I thought of the dream every so often, always with a shudder. I didn't understand what it meant. Eventually I told the dream to my husband's highly regarded psychiatrist. He tossed it off lightly without even asking the circumstances of my life. He said it was not an unusual dream for a child raised solely by women, a child who knew nothing about men. I accepted that facile explanation. It seemed reasonable at the time. It took years before I learned that the dream was about very real fears, fears I denied in order to survive. The safety of my new haven allowed my unconscious to acknowledge the danger I had been in, but I was still too young to cope with the knowledge. I suppressed the fear along with the dream.

My mother had lived with Aunt Hazel for more than a year before I moved in with them. There was a lot of shouting and even thrown furniture when Mother left Aunt Rose's. Mother never did anything quietly. This time she wanted to take her maple bedroom set, the bed the two of us slept in and a vanity. When Aunt Rose said she couldn't take it, Mother picked up the bench and threw it at the mirror attached to the vanity hoping that it would shatter. It didn't. The bedroom set stayed where it was. And so did I.

It was fear not anger that sent me to my new home. I had spent the day with my mother and Aunt Hazel and they had dropped me off mid-afternoon. Aunt Rose and Uncle Jim were not home yet but would be soon. Before they arrived, a thunderstorm struck. The empty house, the lightning-streaked sky, the rolling thunder terrified me. In a panic I called Aunt Hazel's house and she and Mother came back.

By the time they got there, Aunt Rose and Uncle Jim were home. Angry words were exchanged. Mother blamed them for not being there when they were supposed to be. Aunt Rose blamed Mother for leaving me in an empty house. Aunt Hazel kept her head. She must have recognized my terror and decided on the spot that I should come to live with the two of them and her two boarders on Rosewood Avenue. The decision hinged on whether I could take care of myself when I got home from school until the women got home after work. Of course I could. I was nine years old.

The house was another two-story flat, more spacious than Gramma's house. The household mirrored Gramma's house too. Aunt Hazel was divorced and her two boarders were single women: Merle, a stern, gray-haired spinster, who lived in the back bedroom and Violet, a friendly, dark-haired young hairdresser, in the second

17

bedroom. A young couple with a baby rented the upstairs. Mother and Aunt Hazel shared the partially finished attic. They slept in iron-framed twin beds shoved back against the slope of the roof on either side of the room. A library table perpendicular between them was piled with *Official Detective* and other true crime magazines, their preferred reading material. I slept on a cot at the foot of my mother's bed. The area was lighted by bed lamps clamped to the iron bedsteads. The rest of the attic was dark.

To reach this refuge each night, I climbed two flights of stairs, the landings inhabited by mops and brooms and such. On the third floor I crossed the shadowy unfinished half of the attic devoted to the storage of household castoffs and treasures, like the trunk from which Aunt Hazel produced an orange beaded flapper dress to wear to a costume party one night. In that nightly journey, never once did I fear for scary things that bump in the night. The passage was my protective buffer from the dangers of the world. The darkness closed behind me as I climbed up the stairs, enveloping me in a circle of light where I was never afraid to be alone.

I was a skinny kid when I moved to Aunt Hazel's. I weighed forty pounds. I suspect that I did not grow during the traumatic four years between Gramma's departure and my arrival at the house on Rosewood. But that was soon to change.

Aunt Hazel was a woman like none I had ever known. She was built somewhat like my grandmother, short and buxom with no apologies. She went to a costume party once dressed as the man on the flying trapeze, every bump and bulge clearly revealed in red long underwear, this at a time when women wore girdles and dressed to conceal bodily imperfections. She was probably not yet fifty but her hair was white with a blue rinse, fashionably coifed. Her clothes tended toward Chanel suits with chunky costume jewelry, not a house dress in her closet. She wore shorts and halters on cleaning day. She had a deep hearty voice that matched her earthy personality. She said what she thought, laughed with gusto and lived a life

18

peopled with an ill-assorted group of young and old, men and women, and at that time during the war years, lots of young soldiers and sailors who treated her house as home. She was the first woman I knew who had formals and furs in her wardrobe and a whole box of jewelry. She was an Eastern Star. She was not beautiful or even pretty but she had pizazz.

She cooked foods I had never heard of. One night Junket over fresh blueberries in stemmed crystal sherbets, heavenly. I haven't tasted Junket since my children were young. They were unimpressed with it no matter how elegantly served.

She made superb Italian meat sauce with l-o-n-g spaghetti which she taught me to wind on my fork one strand at a time. She served it with tossed salad, literally. She placed washed greens in a super-sized sack--a laundry bag?--twisted the end and slung it in giant windmills to dry the greens with centrifugal force, her effective version of today's salad spinners. She made fabulous waffles with Bisquick--the recipe a taste-test winner at the Eastern Star--and served them with real maple syrup. Every spring we drove to the country in her Chevy coupe with me tucked into the monkey seat in back. We carried home two one-gallon cans, then transferred the amber syrup into sterilized pint jars to last the year.

The first summer I lived there, she promised to bake a cherry pie every day that I picked enough cherries from the enormous tree in the back yard, a promise she must have rued as I climbed the ladder almost daily and picked bucket after bucket. True to her word we ate cherry pie after cherry pie, tart and latticed and wonderful, still my favorite pie especially when made with fresh cherries. I flourished and entered my pre-teen years on the chubby side, puppy fat they called it.

She taught me table manners too. On Saturdays I walked six blocks to the bank where she worked and we went out to lunch when it closed at noon. After the first time she informed me that if the practice was to continue I would have to learn to eat properly. She taught me about napkins in my lap and dabbing my lips, elbows off the table, one hand in my lap, proper use of silverware, not talking with my mouth full, bringing food to my mouth, not vice-versa, and the art of conversation.

My favorite restaurants were Clark's, where I ate hot chicken sandwiches with mashed potatoes and yellow gravy, and the Silver Grill in a downtown department store, where they had fashion shows on Monday nights. She indulged me even though she preferred less fancy places like Grebe's delicatessen, where Mother worked when I was a baby, and Max Gruber's, a noisy bar in downtown Cleveland.

She described my early visits to her bank with my mother when I stood looking down, kicked my foot, and wouldn't talk. Her remedy was dramatics lessons with Miss Shulte on Saturday mornings. Our class of ten-year-olds would parade around the room single-file with Miss Shulte in the center admonishing us: "Heads high. Backs straight. Tummies tucked in. Pick up your feet, don't shuffle."

When we were on stage, she would call from the back of the auditorium, "Don't flop! Lower yourself into the chair. Face the audience." She turned us into poised performers. I decided to be a movie star.

Aunt Hazel taught me to answer the phone as if I welcomed the call. She taught me to take a proper message. She taught me to sew, to hem my clothes, mend them and add little flourishes like ribbons, lace, and rick-rack. She even let me use her electric sewing machine. She taught me what colors went with what--red and yella catch a fella--and what clothes were right for me. She gave me my fashion sense.

Mother, of course, was not too appreciative of this sense of style, especially when she sent the two of us to shop for camp pajamas and we came home with a nightie I couldn't live without. It was a two-piece, bare midriff, sheer mauve confection, sprinkled with tiny purple flowers--reminiscent of the dress Gramma had bought me in New Jersey--and laced on top and at the waist with purple ribbons. It cost $7.95, no small price in 1943. I don't know what I wore to camp that summer but it wasn't the treasured nightgown. I think it was her parting gift to me, although I did not know it then, for Mother had remarried and moved to Detroit and I was soon to join her.

On Saturday nights we listened to *The Hit Parade* and copied down the words to the top ten songs of the week. She typed them at her office for me to add to my collection of song sheets, not sheet music but pamphlets of lyrics to popular songs sold in drug stores. To this day I remember the lyrics to the songs of that time, which we used to sing around the house and when we went for drives in the Chevy: war songs like "Don't Sit Under the Apple Tree," and silly songs like "Marezy Doats."

She also taught me to clean house. I had the privilege of dusting her knickknack shelves of cats, hundreds of cats, and arranging them at my pleasure. She paid me a penny a pane to wash her mullioned windows, providing I got into the corners properly. She also paid a penny each for dandelions I pulled out of the small lawn in front of the house. I seldom managed to get the roots.

Monday nights were laundry nights. I can still conjure up the smell of steamy soap and water and wet clothes and the slosh of water in the copper tank of her state-of-the-art Easy wash machine with the spin drier, not a wringer. I learned to iron, beginning with linen hankies and eventually working my way up to my chintz pinafores with ruffled shoulders. Irons in those days were heavy and did not have heat controls. It was no easy task. She didn't let me use the mangle because I might get my fingers caught.

She taught me to be a hostess, which meant good company, good food, and fresh flowers. My favorite arrangement was a float of gladiola florets in a large concave mirrored disc with glass bubbles floating in between. That mirror and those bubbles are the one thing of hers I wish I had.

She often sent me to search for flowers in the remains of the garden, the section of the yard next to the garage where a few perennials and self-seeded annuals vied with knee-deep weeds. That is where I met the hardy scabiosa, the pincushion flower, that I later grew in my own garden. I love fresh flowers in the house.

I loved my years with Aunt Hazel. She brought fun into my life. She taught me to be a woman, to walk in beauty, to live in abundance, to laugh, to share, to love. She also taught me that an independent woman can lead a good, rich life.

When I said my final goodbye to her, it was three weeks before she succumbed to cancer at the age of 85. When my husband Jerry and I walked into her nursing-home room, she welcomed us in her adopted Louisville accent: "Ah don't know why ya came to see me. Y'know I can't entatain ya, don't ya?"

Little of her body remained as I discovered when I rubbed her back, but her spirit and her voice were as strong as ever. We talked about the present and the past. We talked with joy and laughter. We had three visits on that weekend.

As we drove back to Detroit, I knew when she would die. Her dear friend Charles, who lived across the street, brought her the newspaper every morning just as he had for years, then returned in the evening to visit after work. He planned to be out of town on Christmas day visiting his sister. With no guest to prepare for that day I knew she would die, and she did.

Woody

"Tell me about your father," Melba invited.

It was my second visit to the therapist I would spend the next few years with. We were sitting in her office, she at her desk, I across from her on a tan leather couch. The room was lit only by a desk lamp, no windows. The soft light added to my feeling of safety. I trusted her to listen and understand, to accept my feelings without judgment.

Before the first few words were out of my mouth in answer to her question, I was awash with tears, tears that had been locked inside me for the nine months since my father died. Between sobs that day, I told Melba the story of my father, not the man who had deserted me before my birth, but the man who became a real father to me.

I was ten years old when Woody came into my life. He was one of the gang of people that were always welcomed heartily by Aunt Hazel. I was oblivious to any special relationship he had with my mother but they were married about a year after I moved in.

Woody was different from the men I was used to. My Uncle Jim with his clipped mustache and balding head and my ruddy, muscular Uncle Steve were both short. Woody was tall--at least he seemed so to me though he was well under six feet. His hair was dark and wavy, his eyes brown and alternately soft or twinkly. He was neither thin nor fat but gave the impression of softness and strength both. He was the first man I knew who always wore a suit and tie. He and Uncle Lew, Aunt Hazel's special friend were buddies. They shared a rollicking sense of humor, always telling stories, most of them out of my hearing. I would hear their uproarious laughter and know they were telling dirty jokes again.

They called me a teeny-weeny after a comic strip of elf-like creatures who could fly. They took great delight in talking about an afternoon they picked me up from school. According to them, when the bell rang teeny-weenies exploded out the doors and windows of the school as their parents tried to catch them with butterfly nets. The two men would carry on waving their arms and leaping this way and that until I was in stitches with tears running down my face, hardly able to breathe.

Mother married Woody when I was ten. She moved to Detroit, once more leaving me behind. This time I was happy to stay with Aunt Hazel until the end of the school year when I joined them in Detroit and slept on the living room couch of their one bedroom upstairs flat.

Mother's wedding in Detroit was of no significance to me. I had no part in it. It was just one more event in my life beyond my control. When I married a second time, my children shared in the celebration. How could I leave them out? Many years later when I was in therapy, I burst into tears one morning when I suddenly realized how I had been left out of my mother's wedding and most of her life.

Woody had no children. He welcomed me into his heart as if I were his own and I loved him dearly. In the evenings I would sit in his lap and snuggle and he would tease me as if I were a much younger child. He must have known that I had years of fatherlessness to make up for. He called me Squeedunk and greeted me every morning with a cheerful, "Good morning, Glory."

24

I spent the days of my first summer in a new city alone, without friends. Mother was working. There were a couple of kids across the street but I didn't like them much and only played with them a couple of times. They taught me to play Russian handball, a game that I could play by myself bouncing a ball against the house endlessly while I performed the required claps, arm rolls, turns, etc. before catching the ball and bouncing it again.

Inside I played Solitaire, did jigsaw puzzles, and read--I visited the nearby library regularly. When I met Mary down the street she lent me *The Secret Garden* and it became my favorite book.

Woody gave me a dime every morning for the ice cream man, who pushed his cart through the streets announcing his approach with a handbell. In the evenings I had a daddy, although I never called him that. I called him Woody as I had when I first met him but when I speak of my father, it is Woody that I mean.

I did not feel lonely that summer. I had a family. I was included in most of Mother and Woody's activities: movies, out to dinner, visiting friends. Sometimes Woody did things with just me, like my first tent circus, Barnum and Bailey, and even the freak show: the tattooed lady, the snake charmer, the fire eater and the rest. My mother was horrified when I told her about that.

I grew into my teen years in my own bedroom in the duplex they bought in northwest Detroit. Mother was constantly yelling at me, about what I don't know. I look back and realize what a good kid I was. I got all A's in school, did a lot of house cleaning, and generally stuck around the house reading, knitting--with the help of our next door neighbor--or sewing. I began baby sitting when I was twelve and had my own money for my projects.

When I asked for a dressing table, Woody bought an unfinished one and helped me paint it. I made a skirt for it with brightly striped chintz and Woody made a valance for my window which I covered with the same material. I had rejected a gaudy bedspread printed with huge roses that my mother had bought me.

My room was my refuge. Woody was my staunch defender. He always expected the best from me, was proud of my accomplishments and let me know it.

I can't count the miles he drove and the hours he spent taking me to various activities and carting my friends around to parties and school events until I was old enough to drive. Then he tried to teach me but when I ran over the curb parking in front of our house after one of our driving lessons, he decided he did not have the patience or the nerves to teach me himself. He offered my boy friend the use of his car if he would teach me. When I got my license, he let me use the car whenever I needed it.

He continued to regale me with his far-fetched stories. One Saturday at lunch we watched our neighbor behind us pulling a dead fish from his lily pond. "That fish must have been hit on the head with a raindrop and drowned before he regained consciousness," said Woody.

"Really?" I said aghast before I realized he was kidding.

I thank him for my sense of humor. I tended to take things seriously, not unusual for a kid on her own who has to learn things the hard way. People were always telling me to smile. Woody was fun. He was also reliable and trustworthy. Unlike my mother, if he said he would be somewhere, he was. If he said he would do something, he did. Best of all, he accepted me for myself.

At some point during those years Woody started going to church with me. When I moved to Detroit, I had started sixth grade at Holy Cross Lutheran School. We lived in a rather rough neighborhood and Woody did not want me to go to the nearby school. Instead I had a four mile street car ride--an eleven year old in a strange city--to school everyday and again on Sunday so that I could go to church and Sunday school.

When we moved to the duplex, I continued at Holy Cross only now it was a two-bus ride. Sunday bus schedules were iffy so Woody would often drive me to church. After a few such drives, he decided that he might as well go to services himself as long as he was there. Mother did not go. At first she offered excuses--she had to cook dinner or get ready for company or whatever. Eventually we simply did not expect her to go. When my brother--born when I was almost fifteen--reached Sunday school age at three, it was Woody who took him regularly while Mother slept in. He eventually joined the church.

When I started college at Wayne University, Woody and I established a morning routine. He would get up first and use the bathroom, then go downstairs to start the coffee and pour the orange juice while I showered and dressed. I would set the table and finish breakfast preparations--sometimes eggs or pancakes--while he shaved and dressed. He would come to the table smelling of Old Spice and we would eat together. We would clean up the kitchen, brush our teeth, gather our stuff, then leave together. He dropped me off at school, not far from his office in central Detroit, and go on to work. Mornings were peaceful day starters except when Mother felt she should get up and cook breakfast for us. We finally told her that we would rather she didn't. I don't know that she ever knew how disruptive her presence was to our harmonious morning dance.

Later Woody was a wonderful grandfather to my children. Tim, my oldest, was probably about ten when, unbeknownst to me, he wrote a letter to Woody asking if he could have his old power lawnmower so that he could use the motor from it for a go-cart he was building. My father treated the request in businesslike fashion and wrote back to Tim. He said that he would be happy to give it to him but he should be aware that the oil pan was missing and he explained the ramifications of this. After that exchange, the mower arrived in our garage, eventually powered my son's first go-cart and launched him on his chief avocation: building and rebuilding cars and later boats.

Woody and Joe, my youngest, developed a congenial relationship early on. Joe was about three when the two of them would sit m the living room watching television, my father with his can of beer, Joe with a juice glass that Woody would periodically splash a bit of beer into. When Grampa came to visit, out came the juice glass. It was a ritual.

I have two vivid pictures of Woody in my memory. The first was in the hospital when he was being wheeled back from surgery, still asleep, covered in white, a surgical cap covering his graying hair. I remember thinking he looked remarkably like Lyndon B. Johnson. I didn't dare tell him. He hated LBJ. The second was his open armed welcome when my world was falling apart.

Near the end of my marriage, I took the children to my parents' house in Lansing for a needed separation from my husband. I drove the hour and a half in turmoil not knowing whether Bob would be there when I returned home, fully expecting that he would not. I walked through the breezeway, in through the kitchen door and there was Woody. He had come home from work to be with me. He stood in the kitchen with his arms open and a look of understanding in his brown eyes that required no words. I went into his arms and sobbed. I was safe in the arms of the one person that I could trust.

My father died suddenly of a massive heart attack on Christmas Eve in 1968. Mother called in the morning and said that my brother would be there to help with arrangements. "Come tomorrow after the kids open their presents," she said.

When we arrived on Christmas morning, I hugged her and started to cry. She stiffened up and said, "We won't have any tears."

When I put on a black wool dress for the funeral two days later, she said, "No black. Wear something else."

So there were no tears and no black at my father's funeral. I was seated in the front row of family seats with my children before I realized that my husband had not joined us. He sat off to the side among strangers. I sat alone with my children, my father gone, abandoned by my husband, my emotions frozen, dying inside.

In Melba's office that day almost a year later, the dam broke and my grief came spilling out. Melba comforted me and said, "You need to go home and grieve. Do whatever you need to do to cry it out."

Music helped, especially "Psyche and Eros," conducted by Toscanini. I would play it again and again. The swelling chords that accompanied Psyche's ascent from the underworld invariably stirred me to tears. I sobbed out my grief over the ironing board, in the kitchen cleaning up the dishes, sometimes just sitting in the peace of my living room.

Finally one night I dreamed of my father's burial. This time it was not in that ice covered plot on that bitter cold day at the end of the year. It was sunny and the grass was green and there was nobody there but me, no one even to lower the casket. It sunk slowly into the earth as if by magic and I was finally able to say good-bye.

Wonderful, Wonderful

There were no words left by the time Bob and I walked into Dr. Wonderful's waiting room. I was emotionally drained after days of agonizing, clutching at the last hope for my marriage. Bob was walking on egg shells, not knowing what to say.

The waiting room was sparsely furnished, a desk, a lamp and two straight-backed, leather-cushioned, wooden chairs, a couple of magazines. Nothing to indicate that there was anyone in the vicinity except the light escaping through the crack at the bottom of the door to an inner office. There was a small sign on the desk requesting that you be seated and wait. We did. Later I would find this to be standard at therapists' offices. No receptionists. No signs of welcome. Just sit down and wait, sometimes past the time of the appointment, in the good faith that the therapist was there.

When our hour came, Dr. Wonderful opened the door and greeted us enthusiastically. He was no stranger to us. Bob and I had met eight years earlier, in his Marriage and Family Living class at the university. He had more or less presided over our courtship as we often bumped into him on campus.

I had walked into Dr. Wonderful's class on the first day of my third year at Wayne and was greeted from across the room by a smile and a pair of inviting brown eyes under a thatch of unruly brown hair. I accepted the invitation and sat down next to Bob, my future husband. He and I started to talk like we were old friends, although we had never met and I do not recall ever seeing him before. "Across a crowded room" would be the romantic description of our meeting but it wasn't love at first sight, just a feeling of familiarity.

Looking back, it seems as if we had known each other in another time and had chosen to meet at that moment to spend a portion of our lives together. If it was sexual attraction, I was in a state of denial. I was recovering from a broken relationship, not at all interested in a new one.

Bob and I became friends, had a lot of fun, worked on term papers together, ate lunch together, even cut classes and went flying one afternoon--he had a pilot's license--from a small local airfield. Our first "date" was a class-related lecture we attended one evening. As we said good night he said, "Thanks for talking, kiddo."

We talked for hours in those days, sharing our hopes and dreams. We talked a lot about Bob's troubles. Not doing well in classes, he had no sense of direction for his life. His father expected him to become a doctor, but Bob's inclinations and talents leaned toward engineering. During our unending talks I suggested that he think about dentistry, to me it seemed like a happy combination of his father's expectations and his own preferences.

We talked about religion. Angry at the church and its restrictions, he had turned his back on his Catholic upbringing. He came to church with me where he found the ritual familiar but without the guilt-inducing strictures. Bob settled down to his studies and eventually, with his father's influence, secured a position at University of Detroit Dental School. He also took instructions and joined the Lutheran church. Eighteen years later he would accuse me of managing his life. I thought I was helping him find it.

At the end of my third semester, my parents moved to Lansing and I moved into the dorm to share a room on the eleventh floor with a sorority sister. Bob moved into a room directly under ours two floors down. He hooked up an intercom arrangement, stringing a wire from our window to his, so that we could talk on our own private line and not have to vie for the single phone on each floor that served all residents and was always busy. We had most meals together usually with friends. On our way to our classes after breakfast, we often bumped into Dr. Wonderful, whose eyes lit up whenever he saw us together. He smiled a benign smile and bobbed his head as if granting his blessings on our union.

We were married two months after graduation and spent our honeymoon in a cottage in northern Michigan. We came back to my first job as a speech therapist and Bob's first year of dental school, a lot for a young couple to adjust to, a lot of busyness to mask any trouble on the horizon. We had spent so much time together and talked so much during our two years together that I had no qualms about marrying him. We wanted the same things: four children, a home and church or as our pastor put it, "*kirken, kuchen, and kindern.*" At least that's what he said. I soon learned that he did not always mean what he said.

When we lived in the dorm, we had joined a crowd in the TV lounge every Monday evening to watch *I Love Lucy*. I continued to watch it after we were married often ironing our pre-permapress clothes in front of the TV as I watched. Bob couldn't take time from his homework. Then after seeing the movie *The Long, Long Trailer* he confessed that he hated Lucille Ball. He loved the scene where she fell out the door of the trailer into the mud slough and was completely coated in mud. If he had his way she would have stayed there. As a matter of fact, he wasn't even fond of movies, though we had gone to the movies almost weekly during our two year courtship.

During that courtship he surprised me with flowers on special occasions including a single yellow tulip on the first day of spring and an occasional gardenia for my hair. My birthdays were cause for special celebrations. On my twenty-first, a surprise party with a chocolate birthday cake at our favorite restaurant and the next year an engagement ring. I looked forward to a surprise on my first birthday after we were married. I got a surprise all right: nothing at all. He completely forgot. I was crushed. Every year after that I made sure to remind him well in advance of the big day.

The first major problem we faced was our sexual adjustment. An idealistic fifties couple, starry-eyed, we decided to wait for marriage. Our first encounters were exciting. We couldn't get enough of each other. Eventually, as we settled into our busy lives, sex became routine. Still Bob could not get enough. Every hour on the hour might have pleased him but I doubt if it would have satisfied him. For me it became increasingly difficult as he rolled away afterwards leaving me wide awake and unsatisfied. He accused me of being frigid and started joking about it with our friends. I smiled and went along with his jokes until they became increasingly nasty and I could no longer grit my teeth and bear it.

One night after a party, I told him that if he ever joked about our sex life to friends again, I would tell them in lurid detail about his wham-bam-thank-you-ma'am performance. He never said another word--in company.

It was sometime during the first couple of years of our marriage that I had my first premonition of what the future held for us, at least the first that I was aware of. One evening a group of four couples were gathered in our living room. The women were my sorority sisters. We had been in each others' weddings, were godparents to each others' children, traveled together, and saw each other often. We shared our joys and woes on a regular basis. Conversation that night turned to marriage. It was the golden age of the fifties when people were shocked by a divorce rate of one in four.

I heard myself saying, "I wonder which of the four of us will end up that way." As the words slipped from my lips, I knew. It would be Bob and me. I shuddered and stuffed the thought deep inside me but I never forgot the feeling or the words or even my position in the room and the navy blue wool sheath I was wearing.

I guess I should not have been surprised when the storms of infidelity threatened our marriage after six years. The day that brought us to Dr. Wonderful's office followed a night of confessions and recriminations, tears, rage, and no sleep. I was spreading peanut butter on bread for the children's lunch, tears running down my cheeks. Bob stood watching looking totally helpless. I spelled out the ultimatum: marriage counseling or else. I still can't imagine what "or else" would have meant with three babies, the oldest only four years old. So we ended up in Dr. Wonderful's office.

He was a lovable, apple-cheeked man who looked like the Vernors gnome, bright eyed with a perpetual grin. He sat behind his desk, leaned back in his tilt chair, hands folded across his rounded belly, and nodded his head as he listened to our story. To him everything was "wonderful, wonderful."

He saw the two of us together several times and pronounced that we were like the engine of an automobile, not performing well because of a few iron filings in the engine, the removal of which would restore us to perfection. He must have liked automobile analogies because he later likened our troubled sex life to the difference between a Volkswagen and a Cadillac, that is, that if we had never ridden in a Cadillac, we wouldn't know the difference. I suspect he was a bit shocked when I replied that the problem was that I had ridden in a Cadillac and did know the difference.

After a month or two of weekly visits, he suggested that he see us separately for a while. He and I concluded our visits after a few sessions but he continued to see Bob. I do not know what they worked on or what Bob discovered about himself during that time but our sex life improved, our prospects looked good, and we decided to have the fourth baby we had planned on from the beginning.

I remember my last session with Dr. Wonderful. Bob told me that Dr. W wanted me to come in so I made an appointment for an evening when Bob would be at home to take care of the children.

After our warm first greetings, the two of us looked at each other expectantly. I finally said, "Bob said you wanted to see me."

"No-o-o," he said.

I dropped my head into my hands and felt the tears well up.

"You seem upset," he said with his head tilted down, his chin tucked under, lower lip pooched out, a look of tender concern.

"I am," I replied.

"What's the trouble?"

"I am exhausted."

"Why are you so tired?"

I thought the answer to that was self-evident. He knew that we had a new baby--but I replied, "I had a caesarian section six weeks ago, I have an infant that wakes during the night so I don't get enough sleep, I have three other children to take care of during the day, meals to cook, clothes to wash and iron, and a house to run."

My anger built as I spoke.

"Why are you so angry?"

"By the end of the day all I want to do is collapse. The last thing I want to do is get dressed, drive down here, and talk to you when we have nothing to talk about."

His nodding head did not convince me that he understood my exhaustion. I didn't care if he did or didn't. He probably agreed with Bob whose favorite expression was, "Girls are different," by which he meant that women are constitutionally suited to motherhood. We have a special stamina to meet the constant demands on our physical and emotional energies.

When I terminated my visits with Dr. Wonderful, his prophetic words burned into my brain: "I can't promise you that he will not be unfaithful again."

That was not the last of Dr. Wonderful. Twenty-three years later, after our tumultuous divorce and Bob's escape to Vancouver, my oldest son and his bride-to-be ended up in Dr. Wonderful's office for pre-marital counseling. Not on my recommendation. I heard about it later. Dr. Wonderful, who thought that both Bob and I were "wonderful, wonderful," encouraged Tim to renew his relationship with his estranged father, to forgive him for his abandonment, so everything would be wonderful, wonderful again.

Tim tried, but Bob was still the man who, on Tim's sixteenth birthday, when we were separated but not yet divorced, reneged on his promise to sign over a speedboat to him. This after Tim had completely rebuilt the motor and we had refinished the wood and spruced it up to respectable condition. The reason? Liability.

He was still the man who, when Tim walked into his office to present him with his high school graduation picture, did not have time to see him, the man who, after moving to Vancouver, B.C., returned unopened the invitation to Tim's and his brother Steve's Eagle Scout investiture, stopped paying child support, and had no contact whatsoever with the children for the next ten years.

Bob maintains to this day it was the best thing he could have done for them. After all, look how they all turned out. And he hasn't an inkling of the suffering he caused them.

The upshot of Dr. Wonderful's counsel was that Bob came to Tim's wedding stirring up much distress for my brother and for his wife and daughters--I found them crying together in the restroom. Dr. Wonderful was also a guest, still grinning his eternal grin, to nod his blessing on another union. He probably felt very proud of his role in reuniting a splintered family.

Tim had several contacts with his father in the next three years, which stirred up old hurts and angers and played havoc with his life for weeks at a time afterward. Finally he wrote off his attempts to resolve their relationship. At that point he told Bob he did not care to see or talk to him again--except that he did not put it so politely. He told me that his father was an asshole as if I didn't know. To Tim's credit, a few years later at his grandfather's funeral, he was able to greet his father without recrimination. I'm not sure that everything is wonderful, wonderful, but it's probably as good at it's going to get.

As a counselor Dr. Wonderful was a disaster. He gave me no hint of the depth of Bob's dysfunction, part of which was an obsessive preoccupation with sex, which today would be called an addiction.

Dr. Wonderful was clinging to a fifties agenda of a happy home with a loving wife tending the children while the faithful husband brought home the bacon. In all fairness it was my agenda too. My formula for happiness was an amalgam of church teaching, Jane Lee--Detroit's answer to "Dear Abbey"--and the advice of *Good Housekeeping* and *The Ladies Home Journal*. All these sources placed responsibility for a happy home and a sexually satisfied husband on the wife. Feed that husband well, pamper him, and give him plenty of sex and he will be eternally grateful and treat you like a queen.

It took Bob's second affair--that I know of--to realize that his wandering was not my fault. The realization struck me like the light bulb in a comic strip. I was shopping that day after a visit to Bob's new therapist. I was walking across the parking lot to my car, and it suddenly dawned on me. I was not responsible for his infidelity. It was his own doing. What a relief!

But it did not change my belief in the Cinderella myth. Betty Friedan had not yet published *The Feminine Mystique*, which I suspect Dr. Wonderful would have dubbed "The Feminine Mistake." But even reading that book did not shake my belief that my happiness was entwined with my husband's.

Dr. Wonderful did help to tide us over during the years when the children were too young for me to manage on my own, and we were in no financial position to end the marriage.

He popped up in my life again a few years ago as he did periodically, this time at a writer's conference. Then, on the very morning that I was working on this chapter, I read his death notice in the paper. A chill went down my spine as I said good-bye. He was not much of a counselor but he was a delightful person. Wonderful in fact.

Glorious

"How do you feel about being in competition with me?"

I was taken aback by the question. "I didn't know I was competing with you."

I was in the office of Glorious, the therapist Bob had been seeing for about a year after leaving Dr. Wonderful two years earlier. Bob suggested that it might be helpful for his therapy if I went in to see her too. So I did.

Her question confounded me. How were we competing? I thought we both wanted Bob's mental health. I would do anything to reach that goal. Whatever it took was worth it. I called this co-operation

"I'm not competitive," I said.

"You're one of the most competitive people I know," she persisted.

I said nothing. She didn't know me. Or if she did, what she knew was my husband's version of me, but I didn't say that. Needless to say it was not a very productive session. It is only in retrospect that I can make any sense of the whole episode with Glorious.

The first time I met her was in my husband's hospital room where he was recovering from an appendectomy. I had rushed to Oakwood Hospital carrying our portable black and white TV--TVs were not standard hospital equipment in those days--so that we could watch the astronauts splash down from that historic first landing on the moon. Glorious was there when I arrived. I didn't know who she was. I was distracted looking for an outlet and tuning in the TV in time for the splashdown so I paid little attention to Bob's gratuitous explanation that she was visiting someone else in the hospital and had just stopped in. I blush now at my naivete.

She was beautiful. She had a model's face, well-chiseled features and long, dark, straight hair. She was slender and graceful, quite the opposite of my rounded cuteness. At that subsequent session in her office we went from my competitiveness to the blindness women experience in denying their husband's infidelity. She did not call it blindness. She called it pseudo-imbecility. We did not talk at all about the protective function of such denial: we do not have to deal with what we do not acknowledge.

I was not in a position to deal with my husband's affairs. It took years and years, much to my chagrin, to realize that it wasn't unfaithfulness in general that she was talking about. How were we competing? Clearly there was more to her relationship with Bob than therapy.

I left her office that day feeling like I had been punched in the gut. The picture she had painted of me did not fit my self-image. She said I was a doormat and that the only way a person becomes one is to lie down. I certainly didn't think of myself like that. If anything, I thought I was dominating and in charge, strong in my convictions and willing to stand up for them, a description endorsed by my husband in terms of bossy, stubborn, and mouthy. In much of my life I was this confident person, but not in my marriage. I clung to the belief that putting husband and family first would garner rich rewards. I still believed in Hollywood endings and looked forward to living happily ever after.

I planned to do some shopping that day but found myself wandering through the stores aimlessly, not seeing what I looked at, unable to make the simplest choices. I drove home in a daze.

I had seen Glorious once before in the interim between the hospital visit and that disturbing session with her. It was another curious encounter. At Christmas time I had accompanied Bob to one of his evening therapy sessions so that I could shop for a coat at one of my favorite Birmingham stores. I dropped him off, returned after shopping, and sat reading in the waiting room. When the two of them came out, I stood to greet them and we talked casually.

"Do you know why you hold your arms like that?" she asked.

I glanced down at my arms folded across my breasts and replied in a questioning tone, "No?"

"It's because you are holding in your aggression."

"Really?" I didn't think so but she was the authority and I didn't question her. I was just the housewife, too busy raising four small children to keep up with the latest psychological theories. Dr. Spock was about the extent of my reading at that time along with Alexander Lowen, whose theory of bioenergetics formed the basis of Bob's analysis. I hadn't yet heard of *Body Language,* one of the hot topics in pop psychology at the time

A few years later, when I was well into Sensitivity Training, Haven Hill and the whole human potential movement, I realized that my gesture was a protective one. When endangered we automatically protect our vital organs. My body knew what I did not yet realize. This woman was my adversary and I didn't recognize it, not even after she as much as told me so in that scheduled first session.

Years after the fact I realized that my husband had been in therapywith a woman who interpreted other people's protective ges-tures as restrained aggression. This was blatant projection but I did not know what that was at the time. All I knew was the Psychology 101 definition that we see in others what we deny in ourselves. I didn't recognize it in action and certainly not in a therapist who has supposedly dealt with her own projections before treating others. What a denial of her own power! What a skewed vision of the world.

Two visits with Glorious were all I needed to realize that she had nothing to offer me. But I did not give up. I needed help to understand what was happening to us and I sought it from others. I turned first to Dr. J, the psychoanalyst who supervised Bob's therapy with Glorious.

Therapy with Dr. J and his group was based on the principle that clients are not sick, a principle that Bob reiterated to me over and over. It didn't make much sense to me especially since he kept repeating that there had to be something wrong with me or I would not have married him.

Dr. J's treatment room was in a house around the corner from the modern building that housed the business office and Glorious's treatment room. There were no signs to indicate that the house was anything but a residence. As a consequence I was uncomfortable entering. It was like walking into a living room uninvited when no one is home. There were no signs to indicate that I was in the right place. All doors leading from the room were closed. At least Dr. Wonderful's office had his name on the door and a sign on the desk that requested you to be seated and wait. I guess the point here was to avoid looking like a treatment facility. Even then that looked like denial to me. At ten minutes to the hour a door opened and a patient, or should I say client, emerged.

On the hour the door opened again and Dr. J motioned me into his office, a comfortable dark-paneled room with a desk and a chair at one end and a leather daybed on the other. Book shelves lined one wall. Windows were draped. It was dim. Dr. J sat at his desk and I in the chair next to him as he looked through some letters. I was annoyed but said nothing. Maybe it was a test and I should have reminded him that I was paying for his time, but I didn't. I was still a powerless child in the face of authority. Eventually he looked my way and we began. That day we talked about my relationship with Bob and what I wanted out of our marriage.

"I want Bob to get better so that we can rebuild our marriage."

41

"Are you unhappy in this marriage?"

"Yes but I'm sure that we will be happy again when he finishes his therapy."

"Your happiness cannot depend on your husband."

I don't know how I responded. At the time I was sure therapy would fix everything and we could get on with our lives. "Aren't you angry because of the way he treats you?"

"Not particularly. Frustrated really."

"Well you have a lot to be angry about."

Then we got into the exercise. Bioenergetics is a theory that psychological damage is locked into various parts of the body and there are exercises designed to release the resulting tensions so that the hurts can be analyzed and put to rest. A standard exercise is to hit a bed with a tennis racket to release anger; another to lie down and kick the bed until you break through the armor that protects your emotions. We did both.

The tennis racket did nothing for me. It was too diffuse and the bed too resilient for me. Later I discovered that my anger was more immediate and needed definite focus.

With Melba, the therapist I would eventually see, I would discover that throwing darts at a dartboard which I imagined to be Bob's face was far more therapeutic. I didn't need his picture on the wall as some patients do. Kicking a box full of broken glassware around the basement also worked. The shattering glass was satisfying and reminded me of the day that I had been so angry at Bob that I stood in the kitchen and deliberately crashed three china plates against the porcelain sink, thinking all the time that that was all I could afford to replace. Talk about controlled anger. When Bob was angry he threw things at walls then cleaned up and patched the holes later. Just before we separated, he terrified the children one night when I was out by shattering the TV picture tube because they were fighting over what to watch.

When the tennis racket proved unfruitful, Dr. J suggested I

42

lie down and kick. "Not just your feet. Your legs. Put your body into it. Don't stop."

Eventually I exhausted my energies and broke into tears, the desired result. Dr. J drew me to my feet and up against him in an embrace. I felt the rock hard stomach of the man and stepped back. He meant to comfort me, but there was no comfort there. To apply bioenergetic theory to this man was to see that his feelings were locked into the girdle of musculature around his chest and stomach, the seat of our emotions where we feel empathy and compassion. My body responded instinctively to his lack of feeling. He probably thought I was the unfeeling one for pushing him away.

The upshot of that first visit was that Dr. J was surprised by my energy. He had told Bob that he lived off of my energy. Now he knew how much there was to draw on. He recommended that I hit the bed everyday with a tennis racket to get at my anger. A better recommendation would have been to cry out my grief.

My last visit with Dr. J was a few years later in response to a letter I wrote to him describing Bob's aberrant behavior. He was sleeping on the floor of the living room every night. He wouldn't touch or be touched by me. His eating habits were terrible, odd foods at odd hours, saying that we should not eat when the clock tells us to eat but rather when we are hungry and that we should eat what the body craves and let nutrition take care of itself. He was non-communicative. I was concerned about his physical well-being as well as his mental state. He was getting worse instead of better after nearly five years of psychoanalysis.

Dr. J began our session: "Mrs. K, I do not usually respond to a patient's relatives' correspondence regarding my patients."

I do not remember his explanation for this exception but I suspect in retrospect that he was concerned about possible mal-practice, permitting an unlicensed person to treat patients in his office. Glorious was not a certified therapist. She had been a patient of Dr. J's and was working directly under his supervision, her

43

recommendation being that she had been such a successful patient herself. The irony of that was that she had been referred to my husband for a root canal because of his reputation for handling difficult patients. That led to their personal relationship and then to his therapy.

I had other business to take care of with Dr. J at that meeting. I had developed enough sense of self by then to be able to speak up about things that I had let pass before and as a grad student I was acquainted with a lot of the psychological literature. I recalled to him our first visit when he had read his mail while I waited.

He replied that he had been afraid of me. I didn't know what I had done to cause him fear but I thought that we could be honest with each other. But that was not so.

When I said that I did not understand the games that Bob was playing, Dr. J drew himself up to his full six feet--even though he was sitting--and said in his loftiest tone, "I know that since Eric Berne's book--*The Games People Play*-- has become popular, it has become fashionable to refer to behaviors as games but games are something that we play for fun."

I had done it again. I had said the wrong thing and he did not understand me. What was the use? Dr. J and company were adept at finger pointing that erodes self-esteem. The client might not be sick but he or she was wrong, wrong, wrong.

I later learned that there was a lot of truth in what Dr. J and company had told me during those sessions but they were truths that I had to learn for myself in a setting where the discoveries were a celebration rather than a cause for shame.

The one good that evolved from that session was that Bob started seeing Dr. J instead of Glorious and she drifted out of our lives and probably out of the business.

That was the end of my association with Dr. J and company. I cannot resist including two more of my encounters there however.

After the unsuccessful visits with Glorious, I saw Plain Jane,

44

a psychiatric social worker. During our visit she neatly pigeonholed me as a castrating female and recommended that I be more feminine. I did not buy it--I'd had enough of women being responsible for men's sex lives--but as usual my need to avoid conflict did not permit me to challenge her interpretation. When I found out that she was having trouble with her own marriage, I wrote off our lack of rapport on that basis. Femininity is more than a choice of perfume.

During all of this my daughter Laura seemed to be most affected by the tensions in the household. She spent most of her time alone in her room and seemed generally unhappy. One day during church service, I looked down to see her crying softly. She had no explanation when I asked her about it. Bob and I decided that perhaps she needed therapy too. I made an appointment with Plain Jane's psychiatrist husband, who specialized in children. When I had to change the appointment, I called and talked directly to him. Much to my surprise, he was a stutterer. I knew immediately that I would not be able to work with him. I had been a speech therapist. I was sure that I would see him as a patient instead of a therapist.

"When would you like to reschedule?" he asked.

"I have reconsidered and don't think it will be necessary to see you," I equivocated. I didn't know what I would do yet but I did not want to get into my real reasons.

"Well Mrs. K, your husband is in therapy and your problems will only get worse. You could end up divorced."

"If we end up divorced, I will deal with that then."

"If you end up divorced, you will be in real trouble," he threatened. The line went dead.

I redialed his number and when he answered, I explained, "This is Gerry K again. We must have been cut off."

"Mrs. K, we were not cut off. I hung up." And he did it again.

The Long Cold Winter

During the icy doldrums of January, after Woody's death, Bob and I set out for a neighborhood party. We walked past the familiar homes of friends we had come to know during the ten years we had lived in the community.

We moved into our house a year after Bob's graduation from dental school when his practice was just getting established and I was massively pregnant with Laura, our third child. We had stopped at the house almost daily while it was being built to check on the builders' progress. I fell in love with the community driving through the snowy woods of our neighborhood-to-be and could hardly wait until our move-in date in spring.

River Oaks was like an extended backyard built around a pond in the center where little kids fished with bread balls, carried their catch home in buckets to show off, then threw them back in. Next to the pond was the swimming pool where the kids learned to swim under the tutelage of Tom, our ever alert lifeguard. When they could swim across the pool by themselves, they were allowed to come without parents. We had a lot of very young swimmers in the neighborhood.

Next to that was the old stable built by Henry Ford. The property where River Oaks was built was given to Henry's secretary as a wedding gift and ultimately sold to our developer. The stable became a community house where the kids took piano and dance lessons and adults held meetings, parties, and dinner dances. We had Halloween and Christmas parties, bicycle parades and picnics on the Fourth of July and the annual men's softball game in the school yard bordering the neighborhood. There were woods to explore and the Rouge River nearby. What more could a kid ask for?

As for parents, we sent our children out to play in that neighborhood of two hundred homes knowing they were safe. We all watched out for them. The kids could never understand how we knew about their injuries or misbehavior before they got home to tell us. We were a village. Friendships made there have lasted a lifetime.

Bob was the pied piper. The kids all loved him. Sometimes after mowing the lawn, he would hook up a wagon train behind the power mower and drag the kids around the neighborhood. When he drove our little Fiat to the pool, kids would pile out like the clowns jammed into a circus car.

A couple of years after we moved into our house, during one of our stormy talks, Bob confessed his infidelity and we began our odyssey with Dr. Wonderful. During the glow of those days of reconciliation, we added Joe to the family and put an addition on our house. I was too busy to realize that something was going wrong. Bob's long hours seemed okay. He was an endodontist, a root canal specialist. Emergencies were not unusual. Even in the middle of the night. How naive I was.

I would lie awake waiting for him, unable to sleep. He would come in and sit down in the kitchen to eat a bowl of cereal. I would lie awake feeling desolate as I listened to the clink of his spoon. He said he hated to come home, that he felt uncomfortable there. Home was where he went when there was no place else to go. At first I blamed myself and doubled my efforts to make our home a welcoming place. Eventually I realized that his discomfort at home was only a part of his unhappiness with life.

More and more often he came and went as he pleased. He would leave the house on a simple errand and be gone for hours without explanation. My complaints resulted in prolonged nighttime arguments that always ended up with lovemaking. I would go to sleep thinking things were resolved only to have life go on exactly as before the next day. It happened again and again. Both of us became increasingly miserable. Then Glorious arrived on the scene. I lived in the hope that Dr. J and company would help him to find the happiness that eluded him. I didn't have time to think about my own happiness. I thought if he got to the root of his problems, everything would be fine.

I returned to Wayne, now a state university, in the fall of 1967 to work on my master's degree in speech communication. I had made my decision when we returned from a family vacation in California a year earlier. Vacations with Bob were always wonderful fun times but we would come down with a bump when we returned to the nitty-gritty of everyday life. That year was no exception.

One night soon after our return, we had another one of our interminable discussions of who-knows-what problem. In the wee hours that morning, I sat in a chair in the dark bedroom, exhausted but wide awake, while Bob slept oblivious to my distress. I gazed into the shadows of that dark room and suddenly knew with unexplainable certainty that the marriage would not survive. It was like a brief glimpse into the future, the momentary lifting of a curtain that protects us from knowing what is coming. I knew it with my usual resignation and acceptance of what was beyond my control. It did not mean that I would take steps to end my marriage. Quite the contrary. I never gave up hope. I simply knew I was facing a momentous change in my life. Sadness turned to resignation.

As it turned out, that night opened one of the most exciting and satisfying chapters of my life. I probably never would have become a teacher had I not been propelled into it. I knew that night that I had to prepare myself for a life on my own. It meant going back to school. I began my research on curricula and requirements and ultimately decided that I wanted to teach, preferably at a community college. Joe started kindergarten the next fall and I scheduled a class while he was in school. It was a beginning. It was also a terrific ego boost. I was uncertain about returning to college and competing with young minds. My self-esteem was not very strong after the years of undercutting I had suffered during my marriage.

My fears were unfounded. I took a class in Classical Rhetoric taught by the woman who had been my first advisor as an undergrad. My economics teacher in high school, her best friend, had sent me to her. I loved her and her class. For the first time in my educational experience, I had time to do all the extra reading that I never seemed to be able to do when I was carrying a full class load and working part-time. I immersed myself completely in the material and eventually wrote my master's essay on material from that class. I placed my term paper marked with its red A and the effusive compliments of Mrs. Youngjohn under the Christmas tree.

The next year was even more ego-building. I took a class in group communication and discovered that I was a very effective group participant. Another A on my record and eventually I taught the course, a graduate class, at Wayne State. My life was taking shape and I was feeling hopeful.

Then on Christmas Eve of 1968 without warning my father died of a massive heart attack. The shock of his death had been softened by my spiritual preparedness for Christmas that year. With school and finals added to my household and social obligations, I had decided to remove as much pressure from the season as I could. I allowed time for tree trimming and shopping and even baking cookies. I did nothing that overtaxed me. I did not even send Christmas cards. Our plans were simple and church-centered. We were going to celebrate the true Christmas. My folks planned to come down on Christmas Eve to spend a couple of days, go to midnight service with us and share gift opening with the children.

Then the phone call, my father dead.

After the funeral we brought my mother home with us so she would not be alone for the rest of the holiday season, but she stayed longer. She couldn't face a return to her home alone. We adjusted quite well to her presence in the house. She was a help in many ways especially with the children and basic household maintenance. Still she was a constant presence and the neighborhood party was one of the first opportunities Bob and I had to go out alone with each other since my father's death.

I sang as I dressed in a new wool dress and jacket in a gorgeous shade of coral, especially good with my auburn hair and fair coloring. It was trimmed with gold buttons and chain loops across the waist. I walked into the living room feeling like a million dollars.

Bob looked up and asked, "Isn't that a bit garish?"

I was dumbstruck. Remarks like that had ruined evenings for me before but not that night. I knew I looked good. To hell with you, I thought, but instead I smiled and said, "Really?"

I had compliments on that outfit whenever I wore it. It really was striking. I looked forward to the party. Cleo would be there to give astrological readings. She was developing her persona and her skills as an astrologer and she planned to practice on the guests. I had met Cleo once at a community arts council meeting. She was an arty looking woman with long dark hair and vivid makeup, dressed in bright colored, drapey clothes. We had enjoyed our small talk and the promise of a possible friendship. At the party, we greeted each other with enthusiastic hugs.

Chatting groups had already gathered when Bob and I arrived. The decibel level rose as drinks poured freely and conversation grew more animated. Cleo had spread her charts and books on the round kitchen table between the family room and the living room. She and one of our neighbors sat at one side of the table engrossed in conversation about her reading.

50

When it was my turn, I sat down at the table and gave her my numbers: April 11, 1932, 4:30 A.M., Lakewood, Ohio. She consulted a book and the sheets of data on the table. She frowned in concentration as she pored over the stuff in silence. Then she looked up at me with a forced smile, folded up her papers and said, "Let's not do this."

She rose and swished out of the room in a swirl of red silk. That ended her readings for the evening but later she said to me quietly, "If you want to know what I saw, call me." I didn't. I didn't need an astrologer to tell me that 1969 was going to be the worst year of my life.

By spring Bob was spending even less time at home. Besides his two therapy sessions a week, he was involved with a group of fellow dentists planning a new professional building, arranging financing, and working out the myriad of decisions involved.

Looking back I know that many of those meetings with associates were with the woman who would become his office manager and eventually his second wife. His need for a playmate in his office was a realization that I was miles away from at the time. I was more concerned about the threat to my financial security this investment might involve. I may have been emotionally powerless in those days but I was very savvy about money and I had heard of many women who had trusted their husbands to be fair and been left penniless by divorce. I needed a lawyer.

I called a lawyer friend who recommended one of the finest divorce firms in the city. I called for an appointment and was told that my visit would cost $1,000.00. I said I would think about it. It seemed like so much money. After I hung up, it dawned on me that Bob was paying $90.00 an hour twice a week to a psychiatrist and had been for several years. I called back.

The sun shone brilliantly on the April morning of my appointment but it was still cool. I dressed in a brand-new outfit that I had splurged on: a baby-blue wool double-knit sheath, its matching

51

princess-line coat piped in white leather. It gave me the lift I needed.

As I walked from the parking lot, I looked up at the beautiful old buildings in downtown Detroit and recalled my college years when I had worked as a temp in various offices in those buildings. I'm a morning person and I love being part of a waking city when the streets are fresh and people are scurrying to their jobs. On that crisp morning I recaptured that same exhilaration. Bravado maybe, but when I opened the massive carved wooden door and stepped into the lushly carpeted reception area, I knew I was in the right place.

The advice I had come for revolved around money. I was not surprised. That's why I was there. Later as papers were filed and hearings began, it appalled me that the end of a relationship begun with love and trust and promises would end with a cold disposition of money and property. To the court a divorce is merely the breaking of a contract, of no more significance than any business arrangement.

At the final hearing I was furious when the referee told me that the best thing I could do was to get a job and get on with my life. Despite the fact that I knew he was right and I was working toward that very goal, all I could think of at that moment was that my children had lost a father, now the court wanted to take their mother out of the home. So many problems are blamed on broken homes and children left to their own devices and here was the court contributing to it. It still makes me angry.

At that first meeting, Mr. B complimented me on my money managment that had seen us through the poor years of dental school, beginning a practice, a recession, Bob's return to school to specialize and begin a referral practice, all the while producing a bunch of babies and establishing a home. It felt good to have someone appreciate my contribution to my husband's success. We had spent the first ten years of our marriage living on a shoestring and were finally beginning to reap the rewards. Now this.

Mr B told me to spend more money and keep records of what I spent. With my husband's now large income and bright future, it was

52

important to stop scrimping and establish a more lavish living standard for myself and the children--it would work in my favor in court. He also told me not to go to work because that would diminish the amount of support the court would award. Lastly he said to hide away whatever cash I could for myself. I would need it. I had actually begun the process of improving our life style. We had purchased the cottage. I was spending more on clothes for myself and the children. The saleswomen at Jacobson's knew me by name. My education was proceeding on schedule. Everything was in place but it was not yet time to proceed.

Melba

I walked up the broad white granite steps of the Rackham Building on a pleasant summer evening without the least suspicion of how my life was about to change. Much of my graduate work was in group dynamics. Sensitivity Training was a new development in the field and I was in search of a topic for my master's essay so I thought it might be a fruitful area of investigation. I was the first to arrive in the nondescript classroom in the basement.

The class gathered, taking seats in the wooden one-armed desk-chairs, standard old classroom furniture. Melba and Peer made their entrance; she, an ample, rosy-cheeked woman, her dark hair drawn back in a knot at the back of her head, sparkling dark brown eyes; he, a tall, lanky, tousle-haired Dane with just a touch of an accent. She introduced herself as our trainer and Peer as our co-trainer, then talked about their backgrounds; she, a Ph.D. in psychology with a special interest in creativity; he, an automotive engineer. I was hooked. Creativity is one of my abiding interests and an engineer interested in human potential sounded unique to me.

Melba went on briefly with general information about Sensitivity Training then said that since it is an experiential learning process, it is best to plunge right in. And we did. She gave us a few basic premises and ground rules: feelings are facts, stay in the here

54

and now, do not ask why, do not judge, do not intellectualize. The meanings of these rules would unfold during the exercises.

We began by moving the desks out of the way and sat on the bare floor. The first exercise was to feel our space. We sat in a ring at not quite arms length from each other, closed our eyes and explored the area around us. The very concept of "my space" intrigued me. I had survived for most of my life by fitting myself into other people's space, making do with whatever was left. My first space had been my cozy corner of the dining room where I played with my dolls. When Aunt Rose moved in, I still used that corner but it didn't seem like mine anymore. My treasures were now stored in a dark corner of the basement, a scary place except when Mary Ann was with me. At Aunt Hazel's my space was the attic bed and my company was her orange Persian cat Ninky Pooh. I had the luxury of my own room when Mother and Woody bought their first house but in college I shared with a roommate and when I married it seemed that I had no place to call my own.

That night as I moved my arms about, I brushed the young man next to me. In our post-exercise talk about our feelings during this exercise, some class members said they felt intruded on when they bumped into others, but I felt comfortable sharing my space with another human. It was reassuring to know that I was not alone
.   Our next exercise was a fantasy. We closed our eyes again. Melba described a situation and asked us to put ourselves in it. I do not remember the details of the fantasy but what I do remember terrified me. We were to picture the members of the group coming toward us, but the group in my mind would not move. They stood like stone statues and no matter how I willed them to walk toward me, they did not move. I was not the only one frightened by this fantasy. Mary broke into tears because of her experience and we gathered around her to comfort her. We learned that night how to accept others' feelings and support them.

Melba finished the evening by explaining that the fantasy was our own and that we could control it. If my people would not move, it was something that I was doing to prevent them. That idea was as scary as their not moving in the first place. That was my first brush with empowerment, a term that reached its vogue in the eighties.

I discovered there was a range of responses to any situation and it was my choice how I responded. Until this time I had lived my life feeling that I had no control over what went on around me and I just had to make the best of whatever happened. The idea that I had choices in the matter and that those choices might make a difference was a revelation. It was my first step to taking charge of my life.

That night I gave up the idea of researching this phenomenon for an essay. This was not an experience to be intellectualized. It was about feelings and I had too much to learn to waste my time analyzing it. I started to live it, reveling in my new-found space. My life had been full of unquestioned musts and shoulds. Now I explored other choices, began to recognize some of my own needs, trust my impulses, and own some of my behavior. The cottage was the first case in point.

In the fall we bought a cottage on a lake in Hell, Michigan. I was beginning to recognize my need for space, emotional as well as physical. The inkling of a financial tradeoff of a cottage and Bob's professional property in case of divorce was far from my consciousness at the time. That would come later. The space exercise and my summer experiences brought these things into my awareness.

The cottage was a life saver for me. Remodeling relieved some of the tension between Bob and me. We worked well together. We built an upstairs bathroom to replace the unreliable toilet in the dank walkout basement and rearranged the haphazard kitchen to give us a pleasant eating area. We added a fireplace and carpeted the tile floor downstairs so we now had a cozy living area. The cottage gave me the breathing space I needed and it gave the children a sense of freedom in a whole new world..

When summer came again the first priority for Bob and the

kids was to get out on the lake. We needed a boat. Bob and the kids started the search for a motorboat but we didn't have much to spend after the remodeling we had done.

I woke up one Saturday at the lake and announced, "I want a canoe." The kids moaned and groaned and Bob thought I was crazy but we drove into Dexter that morning and bought a 13-foot Aerocraft aluminum canoe, one that I could manage myself. We brought it home on top of the station wagon and it became the most popular watercraft that we have ever had. It was always in use by someone and I had to make an appointment to use it myself. When not used for transportation to various places on the lake, the kids would turn it over, dive off of it, rock on it until they tumbled into the water, hide under it and do anything else they could think of for water fun.

That summer we lived a life divided between house and cottage. Days at the lake were like vacation time. Bob and I took evening canoe trips on the lake after the children went to bed and enjoyed each other as we had when we first met. I remember walking over to our neighbor's one day, he ahead of me several paces. He turned to look at me with a softness and concern in his eyes that I hadn't seen for several years. I was aglow. That look promised that our marriage was safe after all. August brought us a glorious three weeks full of love and new commitment. I thought Bob's years of therapy had finally paid off.

Then on Labor Day weekend my brother and his wife and Bob and I took the canoe down the river on a trip that turned out to be especially grueling--think the movie *Deliverance*. It took us five hours. We returned exhausted, bug bitten, and sticky to find Mother in hysterics with worry or more accurately abandonment. She would be moving into an apartment that week and was suffering her usual fears of change. We calmed her down and returned to the city. I thanked Bob that night for being there, really there, and we made love, probably for the last time with such tenderness.

The routines of return to school and the obligations of the

fall season and life in general brought our idyll to an abrupt halt. It was aggravated by Mother's departure. Things got worse than ever between Bob and me. Many nights I got no sleep. I couldn't eat. I would sit down in front of a meal and my stomach would lurch. I was exhausted most of the time. My refuge was my classes.

I renewed my plan for independence and the spending recommended by my lawyer. One day that fall a saleswoman from Jacobson's called and said she had something she wanted to show me. It was a charcoal gray wool, sleeveless sheath, belted with a silver buckle, and a matching coat with a Persian lamb collar and cuffs, the most expensive outfit I ever bought. I went down to the jewelry department for silver jewelry to go with it: a brooch and a clasp bracelet set with large gray pearls. It was costume jewelry--probably about $25.00--so I added to it a pair of vermeil mushroom pins and a nuggety gold band that I decided to wear in place of my wedding ring. I knew even as I bought it that it was symbolic of my marriage. It was beautiful to look at but uncomfortable. I couldn't wear it for very long periods because the gold nugget finish was rough and cut into my fingers.

I also signed up for horseback riding lessons for myself and for the children. Riding good old patient Cinnamon gave me the same sense of freedom the cottage had given me during the summer. He trotted around the ring never breaking stride regardless of my ineptitude until I finally learned how to trot, my body rising and falling in the saddle as rhythmically as Cinnamon's hooves tattooed the track, another triumph for me. By this time things were coming to a climax.

One Saturday afternoon Bob called from the office to say he would not be home for awhile because he felt a migraine coming on. He was going to take his medication, stretch out and sleep to see if he could allay it. I don't know why I reacted as I did. This was certainly not unusual. In retrospect I think I knew that he was lying. At any rate, I suddenly found it hard to breathe. I was jumpy and I couldn't sit still. I paced from room to room wringing my hands, tears flowing uncontrollably down my cheeks. I was terrified. I was having a full-blown panic attack.

When I could not calm myself, I called my doctor and asked for a tranquilizer. This seems like an obvious solution but that day it was unthinkable. Glorious, a Christian Scientist, had indoctrinated Bob on mental control, a precept which he passed on to me. Medication was anathema--except I guess for migraines. It's hard to believe that I was so easily intimidated. I called my doctor and he questioned me briefly about my symptoms and their causes then prescribed a light dose of Librium if I promised to come in and see him the next week.

I was so agitated that I could not go to the drugstore myself to pick up the prescription. I took Tim with me and he went in to pick up the package. I could hardly sit still behind the wheel of the car as I waited for him. When I got home I opened the bottle and shook one of the capsules into my hand. I don't know what awful result I expected from swallowing the pill. I had read articles about the dangers of Valium and other such drugs. Bob had convinced me that it was a weakness to need them. With great trepidation I swallowed it. I was greatly relieved to find that within minutes I simply felt normal, not euphoric, not zonked out, just normal.

I saw my doctor the next week and told him about Bob's therapy. He wrinkled his nose when I told him he was seeing Dr. J. He did not think much of psychoanalysis. He suggested that I seek my own counselor. I had already decided to do this. It was time for private therapy. Melba was the perfect choice.

On the day of my first appointment I drove across town on the expressway mellowed by my last Librium. I waited in the sterile waiting room for Melba to appear. I was apprehensive even with the Librium. Melba knew me fairly well from the summer class I had completed and the continuing class already in progress. I trusted her, but this was not a visit I looked forward to. I knew enough about psychotherapy to know that I was embarking on some very hard work.

We spent that first session going over the facts of my life beginning with my unhappy marriage and Bob's therapy, then delving into my childhood and my relationship with my parents. After listening to my tale of woe with very little comment, Melba said, "I think you are suffering a lot of fallout from your husband's therapy. I think you need about ten weeks in which to decide what you really want to do."

She recommended that I see her once a week and continue with the Sensitivity Training so that I would have a place to work on my discoveries. I agreed.

"And next time," she said, "don't take Librium before you come."

"I won't," I said sheepishly. "I don't have any left anyway."

That began a very intensive period of self exploration. At my second visit we talked about my father. The dam broke on my grief. Tears flowed first for the loss of my father, later for the loss of my childhood, the loss of my marriage, but not yet for the loss that set the pattern for my life.

Words, Words, Words

Sticks and stone may break my bones but words will never hurt me. We used to chant that to each other when we were kids. But I know better. Words do hurt.

Bob told Dr. Wonderful that my words were like a torrent of water washing over him and he had only an umbrella for protection. I pictured him cowering under his big black snap-open umbrella, turned away from me with his shoulder hunched, not exactly a listening position. Dr. Wonderful told me to give him the benefit of my reasoning. Why should I when he didn't want to hear? But I did try.

I had spent most of my life trying to make myself clear. If people did not understand me, I thought I had not explained correctly. It never occurred to me that they weren't listening. Success at school and my refuge in the library encouraged my commitment to words and logic. I ignored my impulses and intuitions. I listened to people, blind to underlying meanings and was continually disappointed.

I was used to double messages--saying one thing, meaning another. My mother and my husband used them all the time. I was constantly confused by what I heard. I would hear Mother on the phone responding to an invitation in her cheeriest tones: "We'd love

61

to come. We'll be there if the kids aren't sick or the weather's not bad." Or no one dies or the world doesn't end? Did she want to go or not? Then she would criticize the very people she had been so pleasant to.

Mother would praise my accomplishments to her friends but the message I received was different. "My daughter gets all A's." Making a lot of money is what really counts. "My daughter is in the senior play." She didn't come to see it. "Gerry is an artist like Aunt Ettie." Stop doodling and do something worthwhile.

One Christmas I gave Laura a counted-cross stitch angel I had worked on for almost a year. It was a beautiful piece done on fine gauge linen. Laura fell in love with it while I was working on it. She had collected angels since she was little, so I decided to give it to her as a surprise. When it was finished I asked her to go with me to a framer friend of hers and I had her choose the frame. At our family Christmas gathering she unwrapped the huge box I had used to wrap it and she was thrilled. Everyone oohed and aahed. Even my mother rose to her feet to admire it.

"Who did it?" she asked.

"Mom," said Laura.

"Your mother's an artist," she said to Laura.

She turned to me. "Why didn't you put your initials on it?"

I was used to Mother taking back every compliment she ever gave me, but for the first time I found humor in her trivialization of my work. My kids had already learned to do this. Out of earshot my brother and my boys buzzed mimicking her: "she should have put her initials on it, yes, did you see that? no initials" and on and on in the maddening, teasing way boys do.

A few days later I said to Laura, "Now I know where I got my critical eye. I see flaws in anything right away."

"It took you sixty years to learn that?" said Laura. I guess she knew it all along. But then my daughter is amazing.

"I guess I'm a slow learner," I said. We both laughed because she is also a perfectionist and she admitted she was continuing the family tradition .

I used to cling to words everywhere and could have reported verbatim what anyone said to me in any given situation. "But you said . . ." I would say when I couldn't understand what someone was doing. Sensitivity Training changed that. I learned to pay attention to tone and body language, the real message. The body doesn't lie. Most of our exercises were non-verbal. We talked about what happened during them afterwards.

My discovery of my space and the futility of words that I learned in those classes whetted my appetite. I signed up for the next course. This time we met in a comfortable, carpeted, softly lit room in the MacGregor Conference Center at Wayne State. Again we sat or sprawled on the floor and ignored the furniture, using cushions instead. Sessions became intense in the MacGregor setting, which was more conducive to feelings than a standard classroom.

One evening Melba and Peer disagreed on something. Melba suggested an encounter to resolve their conflict. Peer agreed. It was our first experience with this exercise. The two of them stood facing each other, perhaps ten feet apart. The rest of us enlarged our usual circle around them to give them space. For a minute or so they eyed each other, then took a couple of tentative steps toward each other. Warily they moved together, circling as wrestlers might, feeling each other out. Their facial expressions shifted from wariness to tentative smiles. Eventually Melba held up her arms in a dancing position and Peer accepted her invitation. They danced a few steps, then hugged, and the encounter was over, the conflict resolved.

I was moved by this graceful way of solving a disagreement. I longed for the same resolution in my life. I was worn out from the hurtful words, the flailing anger of my conflicts with Bob. I was tired of the frantic sex that had been our temporary resolution of our differences. We would cling together for a few desperate moments, then move back to our separate corners. I wanted to dance.

One night the group was divided into pairs. One of each pair sat on the floor, arms wrapped around drawn up knees, head tucked in. It was our partners' task to open us up. I closed up first. My partner tried to unfold my arms. I resisted, holding firmly. I did not like the way he tugged at me. He tried to lift my head. I tucked it tighter into my shoulders. I would not be forced open. It felt like I was being invaded. When we traded places, I found it easy to open him. I used the same methods he had used on me but he offered no resistance. He wanted to be forced open. But I did not like to do it anymore than I liked to have it done. I felt that I was intruding on his space, just as he tried to intrude on mine. I preferred an invitation to the dance.

I thought this was a man thing but surprisingly one of the women in the group also preferred this kind of violent opening up. It excited her. I realized that I had used this method on Bob many times, not physically, but insistently demanding that we talk. In his case it was more like chipping away at his defenses until he opened up and we could communicate. Unfortunately I didn't know what to do next. Nor did he. The vulnerability scared him and afterwards he closed up tighter than ever. Ultimately that is how our marriage ended. His therapy opened him up for three glorious weeks but the vulnerability scared him and he chose to retreat behind his defensive wall.

Peer understood the need for invitation rather than intrusion. One night I was overwhelmed by grief. It was during the time that I was mourning my father's death. I had turned on the tap of my tears and I thought they would never stop. The slightest show of emotion touched off a torrent. That night something happened that touched me deeply and I lay crying on the floor curled on my side, my back toward the group, feeling absolutely desolate. Peer lay down next to me in a spoon position without touching me, his body echoed my position. As I felt his non-intrusive presence, I gradually quieted and turned toward him.

Eventually he sat up Indian-style and held me on his lap, like Woody had done so often when I was young. I leaned against his chest and my tears subsided. I felt like a child and even looked like one. The full skirt of my brown and white checked princess-style dress fanned over his crossed legs. I was wearing brown fish net stockings and brown patent leather low heeled pumps with bows on the toes, like a little girl going to a party. And like a child I felt safe.

In a later exercise I returned the invitation to Peer. The group was divided, men sitting lined up on the floor on one side of the room, women on the other. We were supposed to pair off, this time with the women non-verbally choosing the men, who were free to refuse. An older woman in the group had been rebuffed by Peer when she took his hand and tried to pull him up. I realized immediately what was needed, walked across the room and held out my hand palm up. Peer hesitated briefly, then looked into my eyes. I smiled and he got up and joined me.

There was more to my motions than this as the post-exercise discussion revealed. The reactions in the group were interesting. A young man in the group, troubled by his sexual identity, was angry. He accused me of approaching Peer because I wanted his rejection.

"No," I said, "I knew he would accept."

Someone else was disgusted because she said I had used my sexuality in walking across the room. In my private session with Melba, she laughed when I told her I was not aware of my come-hither walk and smile. I had not yet come to grips with my own sexuality which had so often been squelched.

A stiff posture, jutting jaw, jerky movements say anger even when the person denies it. Disdainful tones reveal hostility. Eyes show our joy or sadness or fear. I learned to pay more attention to this language of the body and in the process lost my memory for the spoken words. No longer did my brain play and replay the words that I had so often tried to make sense of. Messages were becoming clearer and I was amazed at what I could see. My life was changing.

65

These changes had an interesting effect on Bob. In some ways he was threatened. In others he was intrigued. One day I told him about one of my fantasy exercises. I had visualized myself in miniature taking an excursion through my body.

The first task was to gain entry. I tried climbing over the lower rim of my eye but found myself sliding down my nasal passage and falling out on to my tongue. I had to try again. This time I tried my ear. My ear drum was like the rubber baffle at the exit of the Surprise House, one of my favorite amusement park attractions at Euclid Beach when I was a kid. I squeezed through the vibrating folds and slid down the eustachian tube into my throat and dropped down into my chest. It looked like a circus tent, rosy pink. I landed on my heart, which was slung across the space on elastic bands like the ropes of a trapeze. I swung freely for a while then dropped down to the diaphragm and bounced across like an aerial artist on a trampoline until I reached a metal ladder at the back, my spine. I climbed down into a boiler room kind of place, dim and filled with pipes and vats. I moved down through one of the drains and found myself between my labia. I could have left at that point but decided I wanted to see my womb so I worked my way up the slippery walls of my vagina until I reached a velvety black cave. I sat there hugging my tucked up knees and basked in the warmth and security of that cozy place.

As I described the challenge and the fun, the mystery and comfort of this journey, Bob was visibly excited. He looked at me with new and appreciative eyes. I was Shaharazade, postponing the end with one more tale. But even Shaharazade ran out of stories. Bob couldn't stand my good feelings. He commented: "Your abdomen was hard and metallic. That's where your feelings are." And here I thought they were in the heart.

If I hadn't just recaptured the comfort of my womb, I might have been stung by these words. Instead I thought about how much fun I'd had swinging on my heart, and went on about my business.

Perhaps it was one of those intriguing moments that caused

him to buy me roses one day. He came home carrying a florist's box which he practically threw at me. I lifted a dozen red roses from the box as he said, "Don't think that I still love you. They were just so beautiful."

The roses told a different story. His scornful tone did not stop my appreciation of the flowers and of him.

"Thank you," I said. I buried my nose in them and added, "They are heavenly."

I took him off guard a week or so later when I had roses delivered to his office with a note that said, "I'm sorry." We had fought the night before and while I didn't feel in the least at fault, I turned things upside down and sent the flowers. No wonder life was becoming intolerable for him. Good old predictable me was out of control.

Sensitivity Training and later Haven Hill, taught me to rely on visual cues and the messages underlying words. I learned to trust my own impulses and intuitions. I no longer had to store all those words in my head. As the babble stopped, I was able to listen to my own voice, that still small voice that would always guide me toward the light.

Crisis

And now the pivotal scene.

If I were to make a movie of this, I would begin with the camera focusing on the children hurriedly putting on their coats and boots in the kitchen of my brother's farmhouse. We would see thirteen-year-old Tim supervising, helping the younger ones and pushing them out the door to play in the snow.

We would hear the crescendo of voices rising in the dining room while the camera pans over the turkey carcass, the pots and pans, the serving dishes with the remaining scraps of a lavish Thanksgiving dinner and the stacks of china on the counter waiting for the sudsy water. The voices of a man and a woman in the background become increasingly harsh.

The camera would shift to the dining room. The table covered in white linen, yellow and rust-colored mums in the center, crystal glasses with the remaining drops of champagne, china coffee cups, crumbs of pumpkin pie and smears of whipped cream on dessert plates scattered on the table. The children's chairs helter-skelter around the room.

At the head of the table, my brother, the man of the family now at the tender age of nearly twenty-two, with knitted brow trying desperately to return the family to peace and harmony. At the foot, my sister-in-law, a very young bride, nearly in tears, fiddling with her napkin. Across from me, my mother, stricken and paralyzed. At the side, Bob and I, the source of the vicious words.

The action: Words stop. I turn and slap Bob hard across the face. We stand. He throws a cup of coffee at me. He walks out of the room. He is leaving.

In the confusion that follows, my brother tries to persuade him to stay and when unsuccessful, offers him a ride to the airport where Bob intends to rent a plane and fly home. Bob refuses. I ask my sister-in-law if she has something I can put on while I rinse the coffee out of my best orange wool dress.

I have taken charge now, comforting my mother, my sister-in-law, my brother, all of whom seem to be wringing their hands helplessly. Cleaning up the mess.

Now the scene shifts out-of-doors. The children stand in a group and watch their father walk off into the snow falling on the country road. They watch until he disappears in the blizzard and all they can see is fields of snow. They walk dejectedly into the house.

I will never forgive him for that final scene.

It was Rob and Renie's first Thanksgiving dinner at the farmhouse they lived in when they were married a year earlier. It was our first Thanksgiving without Woody. Our feelings of loss lurked beneath the surface of the festive holiday that ushered in the anniversary of his death. Now we added the trauma of a new loss.

I tended the children that night as they got ready for bed, explaining as best I could that their father was gone and we would somehow survive. It wasn't until the next day that I could tend to myself and that was with Melba's help.

We met in a classroom, the only space available for our emergency session. I sobbed out the story. As I talked a strange thing happened.

"You sound proud of yourself," Melba commented when I told her that I had slapped Bob.

"I am," I said. "I finally talked to him in the language he understands."

What I meant was that I had stopped parrying with words. The war of words was over. I could no longer be counted on not to make waves. My action conveyed only one meaning. His response did the same.

A month or so later he would say to me: "I never want to feel that angry again."

Bob could not tolerate his own anger. When I think most charitably about his leaving us, I think he may have left in fear for our safety. It had been just a couple of weeks since I had arrived home one night from a sensitivity session. There were no lights on in the house but Bob's car was in the garage. I walked into the quiet house and did not see him sitting in the dark living room as I went into the bedroom. I sensed that something was drastically wrong. I went back to the living room and sat down.

I broke the silence. "Is there something you want to tell me?" I asked.

"The kids were fighting over the TV so I smashed it." His tone was not apologetic, belligerent if anything.

"They must have been frightened," I responded calmly.

"How do you know how they felt?" he hissed, anger pouring from his whole being.

"It just seems that they would be." I got up and left the room.

My disconnection must have been devastating for him. I had always stayed with him when he was upset until he was at peace. Often I gave him a new focus for his anger by criticizing his behavior and turning his anger to resentment of me, much as a child might feel toward a punishing parent even when the child is wrong. Sometimes I absorbed it by taking on his rightful anger at some injustice and leaving him relieved--as Dr J had said, living off my energy. My work with Melba had helped me to see how destructive this was to me and to our marriage.

70

The first time I remember that I disengaged from Bob's feelings, I came into the bedroom to get ready for bed to find him dressed in pajama bottoms, sitting with his legs crossed Indian-style against the wall, papers spread around him on the floor. He was obviously not happy as he shuffled through them.

After I brushed my teeth, I came back and slipped into bed. He began a harangue about his difficulties while I just listened and responded noncommittally. When I did not respond with my customary concern, he worked himself into a tantrum. I looked on in amazement as he banged his head against the wall like a two-year-old. I did what I did when my babies went through their tantrum phase. I waited for him to work it out of his system. Then I turned over and went to sleep. Unthinkable from his standpoint.

I feel as sorry for him now as I do for a child out of control in the same way. It is a terrifying, lonely place to be. But he was not my child. He was a man. I would no longer be sucked into his manipulations.

As he became increasingly frightened by his own anger, I began to appreciate mine. At Haven Hill I would learn that anger proves we are alive. Burying it is an impossible task. It will seep out in ways we are sometimes not even aware of, in criticism, in humor that hurts, in tone of voice and body language. It's also self-defeating. It will give us ulcers or high blood pressure or depression. It will kill us.

On that terrible Thanksgiving day, I was seven or eight weeks into the ten sessions that Melba had recommended to me to find out what I really wanted. I had reason to be proud. Not only had I discovered what I wanted, I had taken my first step toward getting it. I had changed the rules of our marriage.

I would have preferred that Bob share in my adventure. We had a lot of things going for us. We could have had a wonderful life but we could not continue as we were. On that day, however, these thoughts were the farthest thing from my mind. I was a mess of

71

conflicting emotions: fear of the future, longing for the past, anger at what was and the loss of what might have been. I was no longer the child who accepted the whims of fate with equanimity, numb and unaware of my own feelings. I was a rage of feeling. But besides that I felt a core of new power and a faith that all would be well.

Melba ended our session by asking me to close my eyes and envision a green meadow, sun shining brilliantly in a cloudless azure sky. "Breathe the fresh air," she said. "Feel the warmth of the sun."

My meadow looked something like the mountain slope in *The Sound of Music*."

"Now look," she said. "Someone is walking toward you. Can you see who it is?"

"He's tall," I replied, " but I can't see his face."

"He's coming nearer. Can you see now?"

"Yes. It's Peer."

"How does he look?"

"He is smiling."

"Is he saying something?"

"Yes."

"What is he telling you?"

"To love."

Melba smiled a self-satisfied smile when I opened my eyes. "That's pretty wise advice."

I had done enough fantasy with Melba by this time to know that it was my own advice.

"I think you will be fine," she said. I knew she was right.

I walked out of that building feeling relieved, able to breathe again after the tension of the past twenty-four hours. I went home to begin my new life.

Mother was there with the children. As I said goodbye to her at the door, she turned back with a look of terror in her eyes and pleaded in a panicky voice, "Don't get a divorce. Whatever you do, don't get a divorce."

I could not answer her. I watched her walk to her car huddled in her coat, looking very small. I could feel her pain, the pain of her own abandonment that she had never resolved. That day I couldn't help her. It took all of my new-found strength to handle my own feelings and to help the children with theirs.

Aftermath

When I picture myself in the months following that fateful Thanksgiving Day, I am sinking into a threatening sea, gulping for air. A telling image for someone afraid of water. I made my decision, now I needed to learn how to live with it.

The first month with the children was a roller coaster ride of tears and recriminations, explanations and reassurances interspersed with the usual preparations for Christmas. Bob had not told his parents that we were separated. I refused to do it for him. I lived in dread of their dropping in or calling. I am not a good liar. On Christmas Eve Bob stopped by to deliver a color TV, a present for the kids to replace the one he had destroyed. I insisted that he go to see his parents and tell them. They thought we were leaving for Florida on Christmas day and I didn't want to be the one to explain why I was still in town if I saw them somewhere. Merry Christmas, Mom and Dad.

I don't know what I would have done without the children. They filled the emptiness of my life and kept me too busy to feel sorry for myself. After the holidays, we sat down together to discuss the changes we would need to make in the household. We agreed on duties and responsibilities based on age, interests, and abilities.

Tim was just thirteen, the mechanic of the household. He

loved electric trains, model cars, planes and rockets. He had rebuilt the engine he had negotiated from Woody and was working on the go-cart. He was a natural to take over household repairs and improvements. His first grade teacher had said that with his wide ranging interests he could succeed at anything he wanted to do. And he did.

Steve, soon to be twelve, was our naturalist. He collected rocks and bugs and would rather be in the woods than anywhere else. He took over yard chores. Woody would never have believed what a hardworking man Steve grew up to be. He used to shake his head and say, "When Steve sniffs work in the air, he disappears."

Laura, ten, was still entranced with housekeeping, particularly baking and attempts at needlework, identifying with my Mrs. America persona. She was my kitchen helper until she learned to run the power mower, traded off her chores and eventually got her degree in engineering.

Joe, not quite eight, emptied all the wastebaskets and gradually grew into repair jobs. He surprised me one day soon after his father left by carrying groceries in from the car when I got back from the store, something he had never done before. It was his way of saying we didn't need a man in the house.

Each child chose an area besides his own room to keep neat, a system which was only partly successful. They all wrote out budgets to cover their needs--school supplies and lunch money, Sunday School donations and spending money. I established weekly paydays for them. They no longer had to ask Dad for money. Bob complimented me on this innovation. On Saturdays we continued the horseback riding lessons we had started and had Saturday dinner out afterwards.

The changes in their routine were minimal. They continued at their parochial school but I drove them in place of their father. We car pooled with another family so they would have a ride home on my class days. I arranged my classes so I would be home as much as possible when they were. We agreed that they could take care of themselves and each other. They did not want a baby sitter. My best friend lived next door and she and her daughters were available if the kids needed help before I got home. My in-laws were nearby in case of a major emergency. They drove Laura to the hospital the day she broke her finger on the school playground and I met them there.

Life at home was going smoothly. The constant tension was relieved and we relaxed into new rhythms. One night I dreamed that I was taking the children to school in a canoe. I paddled it through traffic with ease. I was concerned about the sharp right turn into the school parking lot but I negotiated it smoothly. The canoe practically propelled itself. I was indeed paddling my own canoe and very well thank you. This dream was much more fun than the out-of-control car and elevator dreams that filled my nights with terror before the separation.

The household organization was easy compared to the inner turmoil I had to cope with. Without Melba, I think I would have drowned. The first ten weeks of my work with her had been diagnostic. I had become aware of some of the problems I needed to deal with. Now I needed to plunge in and work on them. I had become acquainted with my helpless child feelings and the fears I denied in my face-the-world posture. Now I needed to search out the root of those fears so my feelings wouldn't overwhelm me when I least expected it. I accepted Melba's word that one of my deepest problems was separation anxiety, learned, I thought, from my mother's constant desertions and the model she set for me herself, but I hadn't a glimmer of how it had affected my life. I needed to learn to separate old feelings from my reactions to current events in my life. I had to relive the hurts, cry the tears, shout the rage, and shiver the fears locked into my body for all those years. I needed to accept my need for dependence which I had not dared to acknowledge as a child on my own and as the wife of an unreliable man.

My therapy began in earnest. It was hard work. It was painful.

I had days when my body ached so much and my energy level was so low that I could do nothing but lie still and rest all day, allowing all the changes and insights to settle in. It was like having the flu. I came to expect those days. One day I actually had the flu and didn't recognize it until my temperature climbed. At one of our sessions, I told Melba how sensitive I was to everything around me. My body felt raw.

"Close your eyes," she said at the end of that session. "Now picture a foam rubber block the size of your body. Climb into it. Let it absorb all the shocks around you. They can't touch you." I felt warm and protected.

"Until next time climb into that block whenever you need to."

Fantasy was one of the tools that worked very well for me. It helped me to hear the inner voice of my wisdom which was unavailable to me in the hustle-bustle of life.

At my second visit with Melba after Bob left, she asked me to close my eyes and picture myself sitting in my living room. I saw the afternoon sun streaming through the high bottle-glass windows at the end of the room warming the walnut paneling surrounding the open-hearth fireplace. I loved that room. I felt peaceful.

"Where are you?" Melba asked.

"I'm sitting in the gold-flowered chair by the fireplace."

"What are you doing?"

"Reading."

"There are footsteps coming up the walk," she said.

I set my book on the lamp table beside me and got to my feet. I stood looking across the blue-green shag carpeting, through the translucent gold curtains stretched taut in the walnut frames covering the picture window in the hall that stretches the length of the room. I saw no one on the walk leading to the front entrance.

"What are you doing?"

"I'm standing in the middle of the room."

"Are you going to open the door?"

"There is no one there."

"But I hear someone knocking. I think it's Bob."

"There is no one there."

My fantasy could go no farther. There was no one there. I had not given up on the hope that Bob would return and we would live happily ever after but I knew deep inside me that he would not. It would take time for me to accept this and realize what I had really known all along.

A couple of months after Bob moved out of the house, I was startled in the wee hours of the morning by a thunderous crack. I saw the brick wall behind my headboard open from one side of the house to the other, then settle back without a trace of a fracture. I woke to find myself halfway out of bed on my way to the children. I thought it was an earthquake. My heart was beating wildly. It took a few moments to realize it was a dream. How else could I have seen the exterior wall of the house from inside my bedroom? It was the most vivid dream I have ever had. Before I was completely awake, I overcame the paralysis that protects us from injury during dream sleep, an indication of the intensity of the dream.

Melba and I explored the dream the next day. The crack in the brick wall was a simple message. My life had been suddenly disrupted and had settled back solidly on its foundations. Bob's departure was earthshaking but the aftermath was a relief that left the children and me settled and secure.

That dream was the beginning of the dream adventures that became the monitor of my progress and also an indicator of problems. Once or twice a month I would have a new dream to work on, usually the night before a session, and that would set our agenda for the day.

Usually the dreams were associated with insights or changes. Sometimes they were sad or frightening but often they were fun. I learned my dream language and began to understand the wisdom of my unconscious.

One of the symbols that I learned early on was baby, as in

that's your baby. A good friend dropped in one afternoon and talked about her problems. That night I dreamed that I was holding a baby dressed only in a see-through plastic diaper. When the baby messed the diaper, adequately encased but quite visible, I returned the baby to my friend to change. It was her problem, not mine. This was a notable step in my therapy. I was beginning to separate myself from other people's problems. I no longer had to get involved or take care of them.

Water was another recurring symbol. I dreamed of watching overwhelming waves wash against a tall building where I stood safe at a window. I dreamed of picking my way through puddles.

Later it was snow. One night I found myself stranded with my children in a snowy terrain that seemed to be Rocky River Valley, a park from my childhood. Our car had broken down and we had to walk. All of us had jackets except for Joe, the youngest. There was nothing I could do to keep him warm. It was a disturbing dream that I talked out the next day with Melba. The meaning was not difficult to understand. We were all embarking on a difficult journey but Joe was the least prepared.

"And there is nothing you can do to help," Melba said in her deeply compassionate tones.

"Nothing," I said as I wept. Tears still well when I think of that dream and how well my unconscious guides me.

Joe was the child most affected by the divorce. One day when I opened the pantry to an overflowing wastebasket, I had scolded him: "Joe, you have only one job to do and half the time you don't do it."

He brightly replied, "But half the time I do."

He lost that optimism. He went from an eager all A student to a lackluster average, just enough to get by. He blamed me for most of his problems and if I suggested anything, he did the opposite. There was nothing I could do to help. He was nearly thirty years old before he could reevaluate his life and his father, get on with his life and realize his potential for a brilliant future.

79

Of Chairs And Other Things

"For a little girl, you push hard," said Melba.

I had just told her that I was redecorating the bedroom. I had put away the resentment chair and replaced it with a comfortable chair and ottoman in a lovely pale yellow-green damask. That led to a flowery bedspread, drapes, paint, and a lamp. Soon I had a beautiful room that became my refuge. I studied there away from the noise of the kids and the TV. Now it was my space.

The resentment chair? That happened before Bob left. I had grumbled to Melba that I was tired of being stuck with the entire responsibility for the house and children. I resented it.

"Do you resent doing it or having to do it?"

I thought for a minute. Actually I didn't mind keeping house and caring for the children. In fact I found it very satisfying. I loved to cook. I made all my clothes and some of Laura's. I gardened and arranged flowers, did needlework, and practiced all the gentle arts. What I resented was Bob's lack of appreciation for the home I provided. I resented his using it as a hotel.

"But I'm tired of feeling resentful all the time. It's not how I want to be."

That's when she told me to choose a chair. "Not a comfortable chair," she said. "Sit in it for twenty minutes or half an hour a day and

80

feel your resentment. If you find yourself feeling better, get up. And don't sit in it any other time."

I had the perfect chair. It was a pretty rocking chair, one of Bob's mom's castoffs. I had painted it white and high-lighted the carved back and arms with gold. It had a shabby leather inset tacked onto a hole on the seat. Bob removed the leather and filled the space left with upholstery straps and a cushion, but the edges of the hole cut into you when you sat on it. The chair was pretty but uncomfortable, and it didn't rock well. It felt like it was tipping over when you rocked backward.

Everyday I sat in that chair in the bedroom and resented as hard as I could everything that annoyed me in life. I would get up feeling much relieved leaving all my resentment in that chair. Soon I needed it for only ten minutes a day. After Bob left I didn't need it at all. I special-ordered my beautiful new chair and while I waited, the room was painted and draped and the resentment chair banished to the basement.

The funny thing about the chair was that Bob put it on his list of items that he wanted in the property settlement when we divorced. I was only too happy to have him take it away. I have often wondered if he or his new wife was able to sit in that chair without feeling more than the discomfort of that seat.

One of the first things that I had to do while reorganizing the household was to determine what belonged to me and what clearly belonged to Bob. Each week when he came to see the children, I had a box of his stuff waiting for him to take away. What he didn't want, I threw out.

I took great delight one day in crashing a stack of 78 rpm records, one by one into a trash can. Many of them would be collector's items today but I don't regret it for a moment. Before this I had always felt like the caretaker of our house and possessions, not the owner. The separation forced me to own what was mine, including my part in the failure of the marriage.

81

I took my wedding vows very seriously. With my mother for an example, I had vowed never to divorce. I did everything I could to avoid the eventuality.

When I saw what a spineless creature I had become, I hated it but I would not seek a divorce. I would leave that to my husband. If anyone was to give up on the marriage, it would be him. But he was a man who never made a decision until circumstances forced him to so I made life very uncomfortable for him, not because of anything I did to him but rather what I did for myself.

As I refused to be a doormat, as I demanded my space, as my self-esteem rose, he could no longer lead the comfortable life that I made possible for him. I pushed him out of the marriage as surely as if I had packed his clothes and left them on the front porch. He did leave rather than change, but I had pushed hard.

And I didn't stop pushing. "I am going to make him take the organ out of the basement," I told Melba one day.

"Are you sure you want to do that? It's probably valuable."

"Yes, but it's his."

The beautiful old pump organ had been transferred to our basement after his great-aunt Sarah's death in Canada. She had treasured that organ, kept it polished and in good repair all of her ninety-some years. Bob had loved it as a kid it and Aunt Sarah promised it to him.

After the organ was ensconced in our basement play room, we added a room to the house that made straight-on access to the basement stairs impossible. The only way out for the organ was to disassemble it and take it out in pieces. For me it was one more symbol of our marriage, this one with decidedly sexual overtones. If Bob was leaving, so was his organ.

I regretted Aunt Sarah's treasured organ coming to such an ignominious end. But that was not the end. The organ was stored in Bob's brother's garage, unassembled, for many years until my son Steve discovered it. He loved working with wood. He wanted to put it back together but simply did not have the time to do it. He eventually gave the parts to a stranger he found on the internet, a man who collected antique organs and restored them.

Maintaining the cottage as well as the house was more than I could think about at first, but that changed too. One Sunday in late February or March, I drove out to Camp Innisfree to pick up Laura and a group of Girl Scouts after their weekend camp out. It had snowed one of Michigan's spring snows that draped the trees and sparkled the fields in the warming sun. As I drove into the country the cares of the city melted just as the snow would in a day or two. I breathed the crisp air and felt alive and capable of anything. I knew in a blink that I wanted the cottage. When I got home, Bob was there with the boys. The two of us sat down at the kitchen table over daiquiris--his made with lemon juice instead of lime in some new twist of his life.

"I want the cottage," I said.

He seemed unaffected by my announcement. "It would probably be best for the kids if you have it," he replied.

His response did not surprise me. At that stage I'm sure he would have given up anything for what he saw as his freedom. One day he told me he would pay any price to get away from me. But in the end that was not true either. No more than his adamant proclamation, "I will never marry again," to which I replied, "I want to marry again."

Within three months of the final proceedings, he did marry again. It took me three years. There were still many bridges to cross.

One day I stormed into Melba's office. "I am so angry at that man." I meant Bob, of course.

"What has he done now?"

"I had studying to do at the library yesterday but I had to pick up the kids at school so I left early. When I pulled into the parking lot, there was Bob waiting for them. I went home fuming."

"Isn't Wednesday his day?"

"It used to be but I never know when he's going to show up these days."

"Next time you see him, why don't you ask him when he does *not* plan to see the children?"

That seemed silly to me but the next time he took the children, I asked exactly that. He looked perplexed for a moment then he said, "I will pick them up every Wednesday unless I let you know and I will make arrangements with you for a visit every weekend." And he did.

Not only did Bob not always say what he meant, his listening was backwards too. I began to understand some of our communication problems. I thought back to the morning shortly before he moved out when I woke up in the wee hours unable to sleep. I went out to the living room to read so that I would not disturb anyone. After a bit Bob came to the doorway and asked what was the matter.

"Nothing," I said. "I just couldn't sleep."

"Then come back to bed," he snarled. "We'll make love."

"No, I don't want to." Who would with that invitation?

I thought of how often he had gone to the living room in the middle of the night, how l would follow him when I discovered his absence. We would talk about whatever bothered him and usually end up making love. When he needed to be close to me, he moved away. He had interpreted my distance as a desire for closeness. No wonder I was confused.

After the parking lot incident I began to work on my anger with Melba. Tennis rackets and mushy pillows to punch were not for me. That's when Melba recommended that I put a picture of Bob on the basement wall and throw darts at it. I didn't need the picture. My imagination was enough. I threw those darts with all my strength, drawing it from the tips of my toes through my whole body to my fingertips. Then I kicked a box of broken glassware around the basement as she had also suggested. I was breathless by the time I finished but I felt exhilerated.

I lived on anger for a couple of weeks, energized by all the adrenalin flowing through my body. I was able to do things easily that I didn't like to do like clean out Bob's junk, but I finally got tired.

"Anger is no way to live," I told Melba. "I'm exhausted."

"What have you learned?"

"It's a false kind of energy. It feeds on itself and gives the illusion of getting lots done but it drained me of the pleasure of accomplishment."

"So is it time to move on?"

"Yes," I said with relief.

A major test of my growth occurred late that fall. The children and I had had a good summer spending every weekend at the cottage. Now we were all back in school and doing well. Then Bob called one Saturday afternoon and said he was coming over to talk to me. He had decided to move back home. I assume that he had a falling out with his lawyer, the wife of one of his dentist friends. He had moved in with the two of them shortly after we separated. Now nearly a year later he was about to disrupt our lives again.

Agitation struck immediately. I had made a new life for myself. I had new friends. The household was peaceful. Could I tolerate disruption? Yet underneath I still loved him. I believe that marriage is a spiritual bond that is never broken. Disgusted with him as I was much of the time, I still cared about his welfare. If there was the slightest hope of living together in the kind of marriage I wanted, perhaps . . .

I called Melba. We talked about my mixed feelings, my agitation.

"Sit down and breathe," she said. "Trust yourself. You will know what is best for you."

If she had that much faith in me, how could I doubt myself. I sat down, thought about all my new-found strengths, and waited. The children were in bed by the time he arrived. We settled ourselves in the living room.

"Do you mean that you want to try again?" I asked.

"No. I will live here but we will both go our separate ways."

"I don't think that would be very good for the children," I said serenely.

"They'll get used to it," he said.

I don't know what we said after that but it was remarkably like the old battleground with him trying to goad me into anger and hurt and all the old responses. But it didn't work. We were sitting at opposite ends of the couch, in touching distance, but miles apart. I looked at him and realized that the conversation was going nowhere. For him nothing had changed.

"My sensitivity group is coming over tomorrow," I said. "You are welcome to join us. Perhaps we can deal with some of this then."

With that I went to my beautiful bedroom and closed the door behind me, leaving him to sleep on the couch if that was his choice. I can only describe my feelings as closure. This had been a reality check. I saw for myself that he had not changed. I saw that I had. He was not able to suck me into his destructive game. Melba was right. I knew what was best for me. I slept in peace.

In the morning he was gone. There was no further word about his moving back home. Instead he moved into the cottage, a place that was hardly suitable for year round living. I think he wanted to establish a residence claim on the property. He deprived us of the use of it for the next summer. I doubt that he wanted the place for himself but by that time, he simply did not want me to have it.

The next day my sensitivity group gathered in the living room, sprawled on the floor around a crackling fire in the open hearth. We were a group of repeaters who became close. We were meeting on our own between scheduled courses at the university. Melba and Peer were there so we made it a real session.

The final exercise that night was a loving gesture for me. A standard sensitivity exercise is a trust exercise. A member of the group stands surrounded by the group, then falls backward into their

86

arms trusting that they will not let him or her fall. That night we did a variation of the exercise. After they caught me, they bounced me, tossing me up and catching me three or four times. Finally they laid me down on the floor and sat around comfortably. I lay there feeling loved and cared for.

"You can get up whenever you are ready," Melba said.

"It feels so good, I just want to lie here," I said.

My dear friend Ginny sat next to my shoulders. She looked down into my eyes and said, "Now I understand."

She knew how much of my energy went into maintaining the house, caring for the children, and going to school but it was the first time she really knew how tiring it was. Energy was a problem for Ginny. She confessed to me one day that she could probably do much more than she did. Now I wonder if she wasn't already feeling some early warning of the multiple sclerosis that she developed a few years later.

Eventually I sat up. The fire turned to glowing embers. It was time to go. Melba said, "I want to build your fire up again so that we don't leave you with a dying fire."

"No," I said. "I don't want anything left to take care of tonight."

Haven Hill

Ginny introduced me to Haven Hill. Ginny who was everything I was not. She was tall and moved with languid grace. Her voice was deep and soothing, a lovely melody. She had good bones with clearly defined features. She dressed in understated, rather colorless classics, jeans and sweaters for sensitivity sessions.

By contrast I was short and bouncy and round-faced, dressed in flamboyant colors. My first close contact with Ginny was an exercise in which we closed our eyes and felt each others' faces. I was amazed at how soft she was, her skin, her hair. Just like her voice. When I feel the pitch of my voice go up and my tone become strident, I try to think of Ginny's healing voice and lower my own.

Ginny did not like Haven Hill, a series of six weekend retreats at a nature preserve north of Detroit. She said it was too conventional, too slow-paced, too uptight. She liked the rough and tumble of sensitivity training. Stll she invited me to the get acquainted open house for prospective Haven Hillers. The brief presentation sounded like the next step in my journey. The people were all friendly and welcoming. I signed up.

I set out on my drive to Haven Hill on a beautiful afternoon in early November. Dinner was scheduled for six thirty so I allowed more than enough time for the hour's drive in order to find my way on the unfamiliar roads and settle in for the weekend before dark.

I was one year into therapy and a mass of mixed emotions as I joined the Friday rush hour traffic pouring out of the city on Telegraph Road. The late afternoon sun was dazzling. I was looking forward to a weekend away from the children and the new experience, but also a bit apprehensive about the unknown.

As I left the urban traffic and noise, I shook off the pressures of the city and immersed myself in the beauty of the countryside, the colored leaves, the spread of green grass, the vivid blue of the sky. Michigan is at its best in autumn.

It was dusk by the time I saw the sign for Highland Recreation Area, turned left and headed toward the woods rising to my right where the lodge awaited. I joined the few cars in the parking lot just shy of the building, took out my suitcase, and trudged the rest of the way up the hill toward the welcoming entrance.

The lodge was an impressive building that nestled among the trees, all wood and stone. I entered the dim foyer paneled and furnished in dark wood. No one was there yet. I set my tote bag down and walked into the room on my right, a large meeting room. A huge stone fireplace dominated the end wall of the room. One side wall was lined with tall windows. Well-worn couches and chairs circled the room. This was the room that twenty-four of us would call home for one weekend a month for six months to come.

I don't remember who finally greeted me that first evening but I found my way up the carpeted staircase in the foyer to the large L-shaped room on the second floor that I would share with five other women. I unpacked and arranged my clothes in a dresser drawer and the shared closet, then made my way back down to the meeting room where people were beginning to gather.

Ongoers--those repeating the course--were greeting each other with hugs and chatter. I felt left out and ill-at-ease until I saw Hank, whom I had met at the open house. I was glad to see a familiar face and pleased that he remembered me.

The next person I remember meeting was Mariette--our grown up flower child with long flowing hair, mother of six, dressed in her peasant skirt, an on-goer. Mariette would one weekend bring a bouquet of assorted flowers and present them one by one to each of us in our Friday circle.

Then there was Francis, a counselor who had met Fritz Perls, a guru of the human potential movement, author of *Gestalt Therapy*. She was not familiar with his work and when she introduced herself to him at a convention of psychologists, she did not give him the expected acknowledgment. When she tried to strike up a conversation, he announced, "I do not engage in small talk," and walked away. I guess he was as uncomfortable in large social groups as I was.

Soon we were ushered into the dining room where tables were set elegantly with white linen and flowers. We were served a delicious dinner by uniformed waitresses. I gradually began to feel more comfortable as I joined the table conversation and I got to know the people around me. I was glad when dinner was over and we moved back to the big room to begin the program.

The participants at Haven Hill were an assorted group ranging in age from thirty something to past retirement age, but not necessarily retired. There were business people, teachers, counselors, engineers, largely professionals with one thing in common: they wanted to improve their lives and their relationships. This was not a group of neurotics. Their problems were those of most people. The difference was they wanted to deal with them, to make changes, not brush them under a rug. The first watchword of Haven Hill is that you don't have to be sick to get better.

We gathered in the comfortable chairs and couches. Our leader Don sat in a straight chair in front of the fireplace. He sat quietly until we had all settled down and conversation came to a halt. Then he introduced himself. He told us that he had left a successful career in advertising after a heart attack caused him to reevaluate his life. He chose to leave the rat race of advertising and find meaningful work promoting his own growth and the growth of others. He told us that he had affiliated with Shadybrook House in Ohio, a program dedicated to the development of community and personal potential. The Haven Hill growth seminar was an outreach of their program. This was its ninth year in Michigan.

After this general introduction, we began our first exercise. I wish that I could remember the instructions for that encounter but I can't. I only know that the group divided into pairs to get to know each other. I found myself with Hank, I think by his choice. That night he called himself Henry. His "new" name should have been a signal for me that the rules were different for this talk. I found that the familiarity which I assumed was not to be. Social Hank was a different person from the Henry I talked to that night. Henry zeroed in on my insecurities which I had covered up as usual with my brave front.

"I don't believe that you are as happy as you pretend to be," he said.

"I am tonight," I responded.

I had the deep levels of pain surrounding my divorce buried under the euphoria of a new experience but did not want to let them disturb my good feelings that night. Henry tapped into that pain.

Later I would learn that the blaming tone of Henry's analysis was a breach of Haven Hill philosophy. Active listening was a skill we worked on with the aim of understanding the person talking, without interpretation, without judgment, especially without pushing the person to levels that he or she was not ready to deal with. But Henry was just learning as we all were. I'm sure that he was practicing his listening skills and did not think about the effect of his judgment on my feelings. As for me, I was not yet secure enough in my unfolding identity to realize that I was hurting.

After reporting on our work in pairs, we broke into triads. I don't remember this at all probably because I had shut down after my dialogue with Henry. I have only the sketchy reminders in my notebook where I had charted the feelings of that evening.

I recovered my good feelings by bedtime. I stretched out in a bed made up by someone else, with fresh sheets laundered by someone else. I had enjoyed a delicious dinner prepared and served by somebody else. I had spent an evening of community with a group of like-minded peers. I felt rich beyond belief and only slightly guilty that one of my reasons for coming to Haven Hill was to get away from the pressures of school, kids, and life in general for the weekend. I had only myself to be concerned about. I was learning to be good to me.

On Saturday morning we gathered in the meeting room after breakfast. We each received a large three-ring binder with a supply of lined paper and a label for our name to affix to the front. These binders were our private property and not to be invaded by anyone. They would eventually be filled to overflowing with handouts, notes, and exercises.

Don asked us to open our books to the first blank page and list the emotions that we felt and the incidents that precipitated them from the time we left home to the present moment. After that we drew a perpendicular line down the center of the next page, divided the page into positive feelings on the left, negative on the right. Then we charted those feelings on a line that extended from one side of the perpendicular to the other as feelings shifted. Among the feelings on my positive side were the excitement of driving out and the pleasure I felt before I went to sleep. On the negative side were my isolated feelings at gathering and at dinner and my boredom--during the rambling comments--a sensitivity training no-no--of one of the participants. We were then divided into two groups, husbands and wives in separate groups. These groups became our families for the six weekends. Our group met in a cozy upstairs lounge and we talked about our charts.

My chart showed me that my negative feelings were pretty much self-induced by my own self-centeredness. There I was, back to my first lessons in sensitivity training, responsibility for my own behavior. People don't cause me to feel hurt, angry, etc. I bring it on myself. That morning I learned another principle of Haven Hill. We cannot help our feelings but we can choose our reactions. We can nurse our hurts, blame them on others and be miserable or we can acknowledge the hurt, discover what it does for us and let it go.

It was not as simple as it sounds. The hurt I had experienced with Hank the first evening festered until I talked about it the next week with Melba. Only then did I see the missed cues: Henry, not Hank; he the expert, I the neophyte. Our dialogue turned into a duel which I was poorly equipped to fight. I had parried his first blow on a social level but he had struck home on an emotional level.

After lunch and an hour of alone time on that first Saturday, our families gathered in the dining room where a long table was spread with newspapers. A lump of clay sat at each place. The leaders blindfolded us and we worked with the clay for about half an hour.

At first the clay was cold and resistant to my touch but as I worked it, it warmed and became malleable. I had no mental picture of an object. I just let my fingers push and pinch and smooth. When my blindfold came off, I found I had shaped a cornucopia kind of shape that curled in on itself. It had gill-like flaps that protruded at both ends. I don't remember what the others made, nor do I remember any comments. I did recognize the openness of the form I had made and saw the gills as taking things in rather than leaking things out. It seemed like a horn of plenty that needed filling.

A month later at our next weekend we returned to the dining tables, this time in front of large sheets of shiny white paper. Globs of finger paint were dropped on the paper, then we were blindfolded and set to the task of smearing it as we would. This creative venture did not speak to me as the clay had on the previous weekend. The squish of the paints was fun but the result was not particularly illuminating.

I looked across the table at Hank's effort--or Henry's, I don't know which--and noticed that while I had covered the sheet and my hands with paint, he had merely diddled around with his fingertips. When I commented on this--in all innocence of course--he became defensive and inordinately–in my opinion--upset. In Haven Hill fashion I will not interpret his distress but I suspect that he suffered the same lingering pain that I had the previous weekend. I had delivered a riposte for the damage he had done the month before. I am not proud of it but I do accept the responsibility for it.

At the time I was not even sorry for my part in his distress. Now I see both encounters as opportunities for growth. Uncomfortable as they were at the time, we each had something to learn from them. I learned that I can be vindictive and that my innocence can cover dark intent, not a comfortable admission.

There is no way to explain the Haven Hill experience. A curriculum--we did have one--doesn't do it. The fairy tales, myths, Bible stories, and Zen exercises are meaningless without the context of the people. The booklet that chronicles the history and philosophy of Haven Hill seems pedestrian unless you have participated in the experience and can embellish the prose with the feelings and insights discovered there. The Haven Hill experience was concentrated on listening, on goal setting, on getting in touch with our unconscious through our dreams and fantasies.

The setting contributed to the wonder of it all. On those weekends we were a community isolated in the midst of a nature preserve. In fall the leaves were glorious. In spring trillium carpeted the ground. In winter we played in the snow--one day sliding down the hill on baking pans borrowed from the kitchen--or watched from the snugness in the lounge with a fire in the mammoth fireplace. Our bodies were well-fed. Saturday night was steak night, baked potatoes with sour cream, and salad. On Sunday mornings we ate legendary Haven Hill eggs baked in toast cups to the perfect state of softness. There were always fresh fruits and vegetables, fresh baked rolls and desserts. The cooks left an array of leftovers in the kitchen for midnight raids on the refrigerator. Food was part of our community. We ate with good appetite and with appreciation. But the real food was spiritual.

On a shelf in my bedroom rest two objects that are reminders of my Haven Hill experience and indicators of the growth that I experienced in a year's time. One is the clay cornucopia that I made that first weekend. The other is the object that I made a year later when I became an on-goer.

Again we sat in front of the lumps of clay on the first weekend. This time my hands shaped a footed goblet, completely symmetrical. The gills of the previous year had become the base and an unbroken rim around the bowl. Someone commented that I had made something that would hold water. I didn't think of it that way but perhaps in a metaphorical way, he was correct.

The real significance of these objects did not become clear to me for a few years. One day I looked at them and realized that the first was a figure striving for symmetry, a vessel full of openings, while the second was a well-rounded container. Together they showed my progress for the year of hard work that had intervened. I went to Haven Hill searching for the balance that I needed to live a satisfying life. My "gills" were open for new ways of experiencing the world. My trust in my intuitions was still shaky and undeveloped like the small end of my cornucopia reaching for the larger end. The next year I was leading a more balanced life, open and far more able to trust my own wisdom.

Breakthrough

One bitter cold winter weekend during my second year at Haven Hill, our circle huddled in sweaters and blankets around the fireplace. Despite its warm atmosphere, the lodge was a cold drafty place. The fire crackling in the open hearth gave us psychological comfort but its heat did not reach very far. I was so sleepy I could hardly keep my eyes open, and I was teeth-chatteringly cold. I took a corner of a couch and bundled myself into it.

It was Saturday night and we had split into our assigned families. We had no scheduled exercise for this session. It was a time for processing what we had done during the day and to bring up personal problems to the group, to listen to each other and to ourselves. The family was there to help us do this.

Keeping warm and awake took most of my energy that night. I had nothing to bring up to the group but I had a commitment to our family, so when Nan began to talk I gave her my full attention. This was not so much a generous act as a defense. For some reason Nan was suspicious of me. She could not accept my cheerfulness. She seemed to be looking for a vulnerable spot to poke.

Nan was a psychiatrist. She seemed determined to break through what she perceived as my facade and find out who I really was. She described me one day as "nicely packaged," as if I were a

96

commodity. At the time I was wearing a short, red, fitted coat over narrow navy pants and a white blouse and I carried my red tote bag. It was the end of a weekend and I felt terrific and I'm sure I looked like I felt. Her compliment was backhanded to say the least.

Nan had challenged me at our first family session. She asked if I was really as happy as I said I was--shades of Henry on that first night a year earlier. She didn't believe anyone could be so honestly cheerful. Fortunately that evening I felt so good to be back with my nurturing group that nothing could shake my mood. That was not true of my first weekend the year before when my good feelings were far more fragile and my happy face covered real pain. As a consequence of my first encounter with Nan, I was always on my guard with her and particularly observant of her. In short, I didn't trust her.

On that freezing night Nan was asking reassurance from the group that her drinking behavior did not qualify her as an alcoholic. She did not put it quite like that but that is what I heard. She wanted us to understand her need for relaxation after a day of immersion in patients' problems. She was trying to convince herself that her drinking was not out of control. The family obligingly practiced the Haven Hill philosophy, withheld their judgment and expressed understanding one by one until she got to me.

"I'm sorry," I said. "I can't say anything. I just can't put aside my own experience."

"I knew you would be the one to judge me," she hissed.

"I am not judging you," I replied carefully. "I am telling you that I cannot understand because my own feelings get in the way."

"You are judging me," she insisted. Again and again as I futilely restated my inability to comment.

Other members of the group intervened. Couldn't I try? Nan needed my understanding. Etc, etc. I was frustrated and on the verge of tears, but there was nothing else that I could say.

During this exchange, Don came into the room, listened for a while, then joined us. He sat next to me and asked me to tell him what was happening. I said I was unable to respond to Nan's request for reassurance. He asked me to tell her again.

"But I've said it in as many ways as I can."

"One more time. Please."

"I'm sorry, Nan. I can't say anything because I can't put aside my own experience."

"What was your experience, Gerry?" There was a softness in his voice and an invitation in his eyes that reassured me.

I began. "When I was little I lived with my aunt and uncle. They used to drink a lot and sometimes at night when my cousin and I were asleep, they would come into our room, wake up my cousin Janice and beat her."

The words were out. I had never said them before and as long as they were unsaid, it was as if the incidents had never happened. On that cold night at Haven Hill, all my fear, denied since childhood, rose up to give force to my story. I was back in my bed across the room from my cousin. I huddled under my blankets as I listened to the yelling and the blows. I could see my aunt standing aside as my uncle wielded a leather belt. I could see Janice cowering sideways on her bed against the wall, her knees drawn up to her chest to protect her body, her arms covering her face. I don't think I really saw this. I think I constructed it in my imagination. The room was dark with only the light from the hall. They were small people; my aunt pretty with coal black hair, my uncle balding with a precise mustache. Janice was fourteen, about the same size as they were.

"I would listen from my bed, pretending to be asleep. I knew they wouldn't touch me. I was Uncle Jim's favorite. He thought I was cute and smart. He loved me. I never even cried."

Now I shuddered and the tears flowed, child's tears locked up for all those years. And adult tears of sympathy for that abandoned child.

"I just wanted them to go away." My voice was childlike.

I don't know if Don or anyone in the group said anything.

They didn't have to. All they had to do was listen and feel with me. They did that. What I will never forget is the feeling in the middle of my spine--a kind of soundless snap like a rubber band breaking--and a sudden flow of warmth throughout my body. I was warm and wide awake and felt wonderful. I had literally unlocked the fear stored in my body since I was a kid. Energy ran rampant through me. I could have danced all night. I couldn't sleep at all.

Joan our yoga/health food nut, had talked about chakras, the energy sources in our bodies, but I had never paid much attention. Later I heard Shirley Maclaine describe the chakras on a TV talk show and I knew just what she meant. These five centers along the spinal cord are associated with different emotions. My breakthrough was at the third chakra, the solar plexus. This is the center of our personal power and emotional well-being. I had experienced the release of my fear and helplessness caused by the imbalance at that level.

Chakras or not, what happened that night is clear. My encounter with Nan and the group had weakened my defenses. I felt pushed into a corner and unable to defend myself, a helpless child one more time. Then a trusted person, someone I knew would listen, asked to hear my story. I was safe. Even the cold conspired in the release. Shivering can be a fear reaction and my shivering sent the right clues to my mind. Everything was right. I simply let go. Now that the secret was out, dammed up memories of that time of my life flooded back. I am amazed at the wisdom of the child who escaped the sick atmosphere of that house and sought joy with friends and teachers and books.

People ask why abused children don't tell anyone. There was no one to tell. My caretakers were the perpetrators. Besides, how was I to know that this wasn't perfectly normal behavior for adults? This was the first time I had lived in a home with a father. Life in that house was beyond my control. As a child I could only accept it.

In a class that I taught several years later, the subject of child abuse came up for discussion in class. After class one of my favorite students, a curly-haired, good-looking young man, Mr. Personality himself–you couldn't help but love him--came up to me after class. He looked puzzled.

"My father used to whip me with a belt," he said, "but I deserved it. I was always getting into trouble."

I looked straight into his eyes and said, "Is there anything a child can do that deserves that kind of punishment?"

His face lit up with sudden recognition. "No," he breathed softly and left with a new lift in his step.

When I picture the house on Grace during those years, it is usually gloomy. My corner of the dining room, so alive and warm with sunshine and cooking smells and love when Gramma was there, became a place of tedium. When I think of it my skin crawls and it seems that I am waiting for something to happen, something awful.

That Lonesome Valley

Between Haven Hill and my work with Melba I bounced between emotional highs and lows, devastating realizations and triumphant discoveries. Indelible images from that year still evoke the feelings they did at the time.

One Saturday night after dinner at Haven Hill, we gathered in the large meeting room as we always did. Don had an inspiration for an exercise. He asked us to line up in two rows side-by-side--Virginia Reel style--but facing away from each other. One by one we walked through that gauntlet as we all sang the old spiritual: "I must walk that lonesome valley, I must walk it by myself. Nobody else can walk it for me, I must walk it by myself."

The desolation of walking alone between those people with their backs turned was overwhelming. I did not even try to hold back the tears that washed down my cheeks as I passed through. I was a little over a year into intensive therapy. My divorce was in process. There was no going back. I could only go on. The backs of my fellow travelers and hat mournful spiritual were a metaphor for my life.

"You have to do it for yourself, but you can't do it alone," was a watchword at Haven Hill. I had found the people to help me find my way. They were all seeking their own ways. We were there to help each other. After the exercise the room was hushed. There were many hugs but we drifted off to bed in our own cocoons of silence.

Not every exercise was that dramatic. Saturday afternoons were often spent working individually. We would curl up in chairs or sprawl on couches with our notebooks and write whatever ran through our minds. One day we listened to music and wrote as we were stirred by mournful violins, triumphant brass. One day we conducted an imaginary dialogue with two sides of ourselves to see what we could learn from the part of us that we usually do not show to the world--or often to ourselves.

We worked on our want lists--what we wanted to have, to do, and to be. We mined our unconscious for those desires so often at odds with what we think we want. Unconscious wants and fears determine our behavior and often sabotage what we think we want. Sometimes we are not aware of the price we must pay to achieve desires, what preparation is required, what the effects will be on ourselves and those around us.

Don used fantasy to help us uncover our unconscious. One day he asked us to close our eyes. "Picture yourself setting out on a business trip," he began. "You are at the airport, sitting in the waiting area, when you suddenly feel ill. You look for a restroom. By the time you return to the gate, the doors are closed, the plane is taxiing out to the runway. You watch it leave without you. You must go to the desk to make new arrangements but before you do, you sit down to rest. Ten minutes later there is an explosion. The plane you would have taken is completely demolished. You rush to a phone and are about to dial your home number when you stop to think. Here is an opportunity to begin a whole new life. Think of the possibilities. What will you do?"

Much to my surprise, there were people who would walk away from their lives even if only in fantasy. The only thing I pictured was rushing home to my children, hugging them and celebrating my close call. It was not just my sense of responsibility although that was part of it. I was already on the threshold of a new life. I couldn't think of anything more exciting than what I was doing.

Afterwards we wrote down our wants on charts then transferred them to small cards which we inserted into slots in a tri-fold manila portfolio so that we could work with them. For me it should have been a time to reorder my priorities, to determine what I wanted by way of a property settlement in my divorce, what life changes I would make as the children grew and left. That would have been a practical use of my time but I was not ready to do this. My list of things to have included diamond earrings and a flashy red sports car. Frivolous wishes count too and eventually I realized both of those wishes if you could call a fire-engine-red Ford Fiesta a sports car.

I did use the opportunity to try on a new life style. I needed to get out from under the responsibility of the house and yard. I wrote down "townhouse." I later put a deposit down on a condominium to be built in Ann Arbor. It was large enough for the four children and there was a nearby woods to walk the dog. I would be able to go to University of Michigan graduate school to work on my Ph.D.

On the drive home it occurred to me that there was no garage. "Where will we keep the bikes?" The thought thundered into my head. Eventually my deposit was returned and we continued in our home. Since then when I make major decisions, I think of bicycles and look for factors I might be missing.

During those weekends I discovered the slowness of the Haven Hill process that turned Ginny off. We spent hours working on listening, not for facts but for understanding. The reason for listening at Haven Hill is to help others to hear themselves. So we listened without judgment, without questions that would divert the talker from what he or she needed to say, without interjecting our own experiences, without saying, "I know how you feel," without interpretation.

We listened with direct eye contact, with encouraging faces, with comments that echoed what the talker was saying to show that we could walk in his or her shoes--truly under-stand. When tears came, we sat still and shared the feeling. Rushing in to comfort aborts the feelings. We learned that suffering the pain of our circumstances helps us to get on with growth.

Meanwhile Melba helped me to apply what I learned to my life in the world of demands and people who do not care or cannot take time to understand. At some point during the year I got stuck. My life had reached a very pleasant plateau. I had suffered through the pain of grieving. I was pleased with my progress in therapy. I was enjoying the success of my new independence. Life was good.

Melba leaned back in her chair and said, "Gerry, I see you in a beautiful house on the edge of a cliff, backed up against a rock wall. You look very comfortable. The whole world is laid out at your feet. But there is no way out of that house."

I closed my eyes. The sun was brilliant. The front of the house was a wall of glass looking over the ravine. It was beautifully furnished with contemporary furniture, walnut tables, white uphol- stery. There were bouquets of fresh flowers, books, music, every comfort that I could desire. There was no one there but me. I was not at all bothered that there was no way out.

A few days later I dreamed of that house. In my dream I realized I did not want to stay there forever. I looked over the precipice and found that it was not as deep as I thought it was. There was sparkling blue water at the bottom. Without thinking I took a deep breath and dove into cool. clear water. I swam through it and came up on the other side amazed at how easy it was. Progress does not have to be painful. I moved on.

All exercises were not as pleasant as some I have described. I hated it when Melba put an empty chair in front of me and told me to picture someone like Bob or my mother sitting in it. "What do you want to say to him or her?" she would ask.

I had to come up with what I wanted to say in my gut. That meant the things I was too frightened to say in real life. Then I had to switch chairs and answer myself as the other person.

104

I would block continually. The words would not reach my mouth. They would stick in my throat. Before I did this the first time, I thought of myself as outspoken, someone who says what she thinks. I had no idea how protective I was of myself and others. It is a risk to reveal our deepest feelings even to ourselves. It is easier to cover up these feelings with irrelevancies and to accept the other person on a superficial level too. It is also more socially acceptable.

I discovered that not telling lies does not necessarily mean you are honest. I was fooling myself and I didn't even know it. Gradually my self-image and my real self grew together. I began to see distinctions that I had not recognized before. One day Bob said something to me that seemed outlandish.

"I don't believe you," I said.

"Are you calling me a liar?" he demanded angrily.

"No. I am simply telling you that I don't believe you."

He was furious. I had always accepted his equivocations without question. Words are slippery. It's easy to let someone believe what they want to believe. This time he could not shift the focus to my name calling. In the face of my unaccusing statement, there was no room for denials. Whether he was lying or not was irrelevant. I did not believe him and that was a fact he had little control over. No wonder he was angry.

I was also learning to accept differences of opinion in a new way. I often thought of the truths of the world as black and white, right or wrong. I found that being right does not make someone else wrong. It usually means that we see things differently. This gave me new peace of mind. I did not have to defend my views or challenge others.

One evening at Haven Hill, Marriette calmly said to me, "I am really angry that you . . ."

I don't recall what I had said or done.

"I can see why you are," I replied and we went on from there. No accusations. No apologies. No defenses. A difference that we could live with. We appreciated each other.

I learned to recognize with serenity what I could do nothing about. One morning Steve was in a total snit because he had no clean jeans to wear to school. I sat at the table with my coffee as he stormed up from the laundry room yelling at me for not doing the wash. I did not point out, as I might have at one time, that he had used the floor of his bedroom for a laundry basket. There was nothing I could do to produce clean jeans but I could keep from making the situation worse with accusations. Soon he came to breakfast in a calmer mood, dressed suitably for school.

I discovered that year that I was not the extrovert that I thought I was. I am an ambivert, capable of outgoingness when the situation calls for it, but generally turning inward and far more contemplative than I knew.

I became comfortable with my new self. I was more relaxed. Don commented one day that my face had softened. The tension he had seen there when we first met was gone. All that growth was reflected in the clay chalice I formed on the first weekend of my second year at Haven Hill.

Gramma

Years ago there was a Kellogg's commercial on television that captivated me every time I watched it. A long harvest table set with cereal bowls stood in a field of ripe wheat. A group of smiling children and adults stretched down both sides of the table singing the glories of shredded wheat. I was entranced by the second figure on the right.

Every time that person stood up to sing a two-line solo, I would stare greedily at the broad face, full lips, gray hair, and the nightshirt on the short stocky body, just like one my grandmother wore every night as she brushed her beautiful hair and read the Bible to me. It was my grandmother! Except that after a while I realized it was a man. Still I continued to watch every time I saw it with rapt concentration on that figure. If it were still played I'm sure I would watch that way again.

My grandmother was the key element that three years of therapy had led to. My breakthrough at Haven Hill had opened up the Pandora's box of those years after her departure. Soon afterwards I began dealing with the feelings surrounding her absence.

Melba and I had talked about my separation anxiety which I had attributed it to my early experiences with my mother's repeated desertions. I had no idea that my grandmother's leaving affected me so drastically. But deep inside, beyond my awareness, I yearned for her. That face in the commercial stirred that yearning.

A dream heralded the revelation of my grandmother's importance in my life. It was probably the most detailed dream I have ever had. Melba and I explored each detail.

I was driving Bob's Mercedes 90SL--a car I hated to drive. Joe and his dad had shared many adventures in that car on "bumming day," Bob's day off, when I bowled with a women's league and the two of them were on their own. In my dream, Joe was in the front seat next to me and the top was down as it often was when the two of them went off together. I pulled into the drive of Bob's cousin Rosemary's house a few blocks down the street from the duplex where we lived when we were first married. I left Joe in the car while I went into the house. The living room had been rearranged with couches and chairs lined up on all four walls like a waiting room. There were babies--my dream symbol for problems--lying side-by-side in every space. All the babies were deformed. I looked around horrified. The babies were Bob's, and his office manager was in charge of them. She came through the arch from the bedroom dressed in a granny gown. She had long straight hair that fell to her knees. It had been clipped about an inch up from its ends and the clippings clung to her flannel gown. I was there to deliver a package I had left in the trunk of the car. It was an awkward bundle wrapped in brown paper, tied with cord.

"Describe it to me," Melba said.

"It was long and lumpy."

"How long?" asked Melba.

"It filled the width of the trunk. It was floppy and too heavy for me to pick up."

"Like a body?"

"Could be."

We went on to talk about the other details in Gestalt fashion with me taking the part of each element in the dream. I became the

108

car, the bundle, the clipped ends of hair. For the first time ever Melba gave me her interpretation of the symbols I didn't understand. I was astounded at how right she was.

"I think the package could be your grandmother."

I had to unwrap that bundle in order to understand Gramma's place in my life, the last task of my therapy. Melba suggested that the hair clippings indicated that I was near the end. I had only those loose ends to brush away and those were attached to the granny gown, my right brain's way of telling me that all I needed to do yet was explore my relationship with my grandmother. And so we talked about her.

"What do you want to say to her?" Melba asked.

There was that chair in front of me again. "I don't know," I said in tears. I couldn't say anything. I was the child she had left without so much as a goodbye. I had no words at the time she left and no words to deal with it that day in Melba's office.

"How often did you see your grandmother after she left?" Melba asked.

"I visited her twice in New Jersey."

"What do you remember about those visits?"

The first summer she was gone, Aunt Rose and I took the train to visit Gramma and meet her new husband. I remember eating sandwiches that Aunt Rose had packed for lunch on the train.

The house stood on a steep rise with cement steps leading up from the sidewalk to the front door, but nobody used that door. The back door opened level with the drive at the back of the house. That was the door we used. It led into the kitchen where we spent our first evening, gathered around the table drinking Grandpa Hartos's homemade wine. Everyone was laughing and talking Slovak. I was sitting on Gramma's lap, happy to be there. Nobody noticed how many sips of sour wine I had from her glass. When I went to bed, the room rocked and the bed spun and I felt awful.

In the morning I played under the grape arbors in the side

yard. The house was built on one lot of a two-lot parcel. The other lot was garden and rows of grape vines. I loved running through the tunnels of vines and leaves where no one could see me.

Gramma took me to the candy store across the street on the corner and gave me some pennies to spend. I bought sugary white cigarettes with painted red tips and pastel buttons stuck to long strips of paper and jujubes, all my favorites.

One day Gramma took me downtown shopping and bought me two dresses that I picked out. One was a navy blue middy with a sailor collar trimmed with white braid and gold star buttons. Its skirt was red and white striped pleats. The other was mauve sprinkled with flowers with a skirt that whirled above my pants when I twirled.

As I wrote this it occurred to me that the color and the print were similar to the nightie Aunt Hazel and I had bought a few years later instead of the camping pajamas we were supposed to buy. Mauve is still one of my favorite colors. Mother hated both dresses on sight. I loved them..

The next year Mother and I drove to New Jersey with my uncle Frank, my biological father's brother-in-law and my favorite uncle who always gave me money for comic books when we visited him. The first night on the road we stayed in a tourist cabin where Mother hung a blanket or a sheet between the bed she and I slept in and the one Uncle Frank slept in. It was hot and steamy in the cabin when we woke up. I was surprised when I went outside that it was foggy and chilly. I had never seen mountains before and with the leaves changing colors they were beautiful.

In New Jersey I stayed alone with Gramma most of the time while Mother and Uncle Frank went to the World's Fair in New York City. I wanted to go with them but didn't really mind staying with Gramma.

I did spend one day in the city with them. I ice skated at Rockefeller Center while they watched. Then I got separated from them as we walked through the plaza leading to Fifth Avenue. All I

110

could see were the legs of rushing people and the bright yellow flowers in the planters. A few moments of terror and there was Mother's hand. I was safe. I capped the day by throwing up on a tour bus and swallowing a glug of milk of magnesia that Mother managed to buy somewhere. So much for the big city. After that I happily stayed with Gramma while they went sightseeing.

I saw Gramma again when I was a teenager and she had moved back to the upper flat on Grace Avenue. The visit was strained as a first visit with a stranger would be. The next time I went to see her, Aunt Rose said she wouldn't even know me and I shouldn't go up.

"How did you feel when she died?"

"I didn't feel anything. I didn't know her. Bob's grandmother had died the same day. We went to her funeral one day in Detroit, then drove to Lakewood and stayed in a motel for Gramma's funeral the next morning. Tim was ten months old. I was busy with diapers and baby food. I remember Tim crying during the funeral service and my aunt glaring at me so I took him out to the hall. I didn't have time to think about myself."

Feelings and words came in a dream a few days later when I watched my fully grown self in miniature calling after my grandmother as she was leaving, "Take me with you. Take me with you."

I woke in tears, tears stored for all those years, tears for that young child left on her own in a world of troubled adults with no one to turn to for comfort or understanding. So just as I had buried my father in a dream when I was ready to say goodbye, I now accepted my grandmother's abandonment and knew why I felt like a helpless child for so much of my life.

A few months later, it was time to say goodbye to Melba. By that time we were meeting in the sunny morning room of the old mansion in Indian Village that she and her husband had bought. She had chosen that windowed, east-facing room for her office. We sat in comfy chairs facing each other, no desk to interfere. She some-

111

times served me tea with honey. An old German shepherd came with the house and she lay at my feet during our sessions.

On that last day, I brought a book that I had borrowed to return to Melba. As I sat down in my chair, I noticed that on the end table next to her chair was a paper I had written that she was returning to me.

"How did you know?" I asked.

That knowing smile played about her lips and her dark eyes sparkled. "It was time," she said.

We parted with hugs and good wishes. Of course I saw her many times after that, at Haven Hill, at workshops, seminars and lectures. But that was the end of our therapeutic relationship. We had finished our work together. Now we could be friends.

It would be many more years before I asked the question that seems so obvious to me now. Why didn't I see my grandmother for all those years? I have only a few hints at the answer.

After my recovery of those lost years, I wrote a reminiscence of my life with Gramma. Eventually it was published in an anthology of works by Dearborn writers and I sent a copy to my mother. It was a loving piece of prose/poetry. The next time I saw Mother, she said in tones laden with bitterness, "I could tell you some stories about your grandmother." I closed my ears and said, "I don't want to hear them."

At the time I could not tolerate anything negative about my rediscovered gramma. I know now that I should have asked why I never saw her as I was growing up, why I had no letters, no cards, no gifts. I finally did ask about her years later, but Mother responded with anger and defensiveness. There was no point in pursuing the question.

It is too late now ever to know. But that is better than the slightest chance that Gramma didn't love me as much as I think she did. It is better to believe that times were different then. Travel was expensive and we didn't have much money. Gramma may not have been able to write in English. We didn't have a phone and long distance calls were not as freely made as they are today. Any excuse will do.

No matter. I had those five years of her love and care. They gave me the faith, the strength, and the self-esteem to search my soul and face the world whatever it might bring.

On My Own

Completing therapy was like graduating from high school. I had the tools to cope with life, now I had to use them.

Rummaging through the past had unearthed the roots of my fears and helplessness. I had opened the wound of grief that lay under the anger and hostility I so often felt. I had discovered a core of sadness, sadness for the separation I felt from others and the yearning for connection. I came to understand the root of all my sadness to be separation from God, the banishment from the garden of Eden, the longing to return. This gave me much needed serenity.

Dreams continued to monitor my life. One day the forensics chairman of the speech department called me into his office and offered me the opportunity to coach students for individual events at speech contests. I told him I needed to think about it and left his office elated by the offer. It was a glowing affirmation of my work in grad school, an opportunity many grad assistants would die for. It would not only look great on my resume, it would give me a new network of job contacts because it would involve traveling to other colleges for the contests. Besides that, I loved to work with students one-on-one. But there were problems. My schedule would be unpredictable because I would have to accommodate the students' schedules. Who would take charge of my kids when I was away?

That night I dreamed that I was driving into the parking structure at the university. I drove up the ramp and shifted into reverse to back into a parking space. When I applied the brake, the car continued its backward path down the slope of the ramp, off the edge, into water. Then I was in the back seat of the car. Water was rising around me. I could not open the door. I remembered hearing that in a situation like that you had to wait until the car filled with water so that the pressure inside and outside the car equalized and the door would open. I was remarkably calm as the water rose around me. "I will either make it or I won't," I thought.

Then I woke up, not frightened, but I knew that I had to turn down the job. I would be getting in over my head and not be able to control my life. I've often wondered how my life would have turned out had I accepted the position, but I never regretted it. Thank goodness for all that dream work!

The major test of the lessons learned in therapy arrived shortly after the new year in 1974. I had visited my dentist, a long time friend. He was Bob's mentor when he was in dental school and referred many patients to Bob for root canals. After examining my teeth he invited me into his private office.

"Do you know where Bob is?" he asked.

I was puzzled by the question.

"I haven't been able to reach him. His phone has been disconnected and his office is empty"

I can't imagine what I responded.

"I thought you should know," he said in a concerned voice.

I went home in a daze. I don't know who I talked to that day but I finally ascertained that Bob had indeed disappeared. The last person I called was a friend who recognized my distress.

"Call his parents," she said. "Call them." She was emphatic.

I didn't know what good they would be but I did call. My father-in-law arrived shortly, black bag in hand. He disclaimed any knowledge of Bob's leaving or his whereabouts. He opened his bag and took out a syringe. His solution to my near hysteria was a sedative! I refused. He left.

If I learned nothing else during my years of therapy, it was that running away from reality seldom helps and usually makes things worse. I was not about to bury this abandonment as I had buried all my childhood abandonments. I had the tools to cope with this one. What I needed was someone to be with me. I called Jerry, my husband to be although I did not know it then. He and I had worked through our disintegrating marriages together. He would help me.

Jerry and I had met in my third Sensitivity Training class, his first. On the first evening the group was divided in two: new-comers, the out group, and repeaters, the in group. We then paired off one-to-one from each group to introduce ourselves. We were to explore how it feels to be "in" or "out." Before I even looked around, a short, well-muscled man popped up in front of me. He had dark wavy hair and brown puppy-dog eyes

"What is this stuff all about?" he asked.

It was my first chance to practice a major lesson. I did not have to be a teacher in every situation. I didn't have to tell everything I knew. In this case I'm not sure I knew anyway, certainly not well enough to explain.

"I don't know," I responded with a Mona Lisa smile. "It is something you have to discover for yourself."

We still laugh about that introduction. It piqued his curiosity. I was a challenge. We partnered often from then on, dealing in exercises with what we could not deal with in our marriages, discovering our own contributions to our failures, and discovering what we wanted in a relationship. We rebounded into each other's arms, each finding in the other what we did not have in our spouses. Eventually we married.

Jerry came over immediately on that dreadful night. He held me until I finally fell asleep. In the morning I pulled myself together

116

as best I could. I suppressed my jumpiness and went about my business of the day. Teaching my classes was not a great problem. I stayed with the here and now of the classroom. Studying was something else. Greek translation was impossible. I explained my state to my professor, a dear woman who would later serve on my graduate committee, and asked her for a few days grace from homework. She not only granted that but offered to help in any way she could. "Including money," she said.

I told a few associates what had happened. Two of them volunteered to nose around and see what they could find out. They visited Bob's office and talked to people in the building. Their efforts were futile other than to confirm that his flight surprised everybody and no one knew where he had gone. He left a trail of destruction, however. He was unhappy with the price he had received for his share of the building and smashed the custom plumbing fixtures in the bathroom of his suite. Shades of Mother and the vanity at Aunt Rose's!

In the next few days as I sorted out the realities of my situation, my first priority was money. I knew I did not have enough to keep us afloat for long and I had a contract to teach until June which limited the immediate possibilities of increasing my income. I saw no recourse but to borrow. I went to Bob's parents. The brief visit was surreal. I explained the situation and told them I would have to sell the house but that would take time. If I could borrow enough money to get through June, we would probably be able to make it.

Their answer? "Well, we're living on social security now. We just can't do that."

Bob's dad was a surgeon in practice into his seventies. If he didn't have over a million dollars stashed away in investments, he must have been the worst money manager in history.

My mother-in-law changed the subject. "What do you think of Nixon?" she chirped.

Watergate was unfolding at the time. I couldn't believe my

ears. My life and the lives of her grandchildren were in a shambles and she wanted to talk politics? I got out of there as soon as I could. At the door with a sweet smile she said, "You might have to marry again."

I didn't know whether to laugh or cry. This final rejection might have been devastating were it not for all the work I had done with Melba and at Haven Hill. Before I went to see them, I had written a short-short story in which an abandoned mother asks her in-laws for food for her hungry children. They serve her tea and give her leftover cake to take home. The story showed that I knew deep down my in-laws would not loan me the money even before I asked. What is surprising is that I also knew how irrelevant their response would be. The characters in my story did not mention Nixon but the dialogue was flighty and non- responsive as my mother-in-law's was in fact. When I got home, I called Jerry and told him what had happened.

"How much money do you need?" he asked.

"I need fifty dollars a week," I replied. I had carefully computed our bare needs down to the penny. I had been collecting $200.00 per week in child support. Now I wouldn't have that and I had to come up with an additional $100.00 a month to take over the cottage payments which Bob had been ordered to pay as part of our property settlement. I would also have to pay the children's medical costs and insurance.

Jerry said, "I will pay you that if you will feed me dinners every night."

He was separated from his wife and sharing a house with a friend living a few miles away. He had been joining us for a couple of meals every week. I jumped at the offer. We would survive.

A month or so later an article appeared in the Sunday paper about a skip tracer named Victor Boner. I couldn't have chosen a better name for him if he were a fictional character in one of my short stories. He had found people in faraway places without ever leaving his office in Mt. Clemens. He accomplished this for the nominal cost of $50.00. I could not afford a private investigator but I could afford that. On Monday between classes I drove out to see him at his office.

He sat behind his cluttered desk in a nondescript one-room office as I told him my story: Bob was an endodontist. He had disappeared sometime around the beginning of the year without leaving a forwarding address. A friend of mine at bridge club had said that she had heard another dentist mention that he had moved to Vancouver, B.C.

Mr. Boner responded: "He is a professional man. He will be practicing his profession wherever he goes. Men don't usually give up their creature comforts to comb beaches. He will be licensed and listed with his professional organization."

"The American Association of Endondontists," I said.

We talked for a while about how he worked. "People have so many records of business with utilities, banks, and the government. All you have to do is check into those records. If you really want to disappear, just move three times in a short period of time, even in the same neighborhood, and they'll never find you," he said.

He told me that he has a lot of phone contacts and that you can get an amazing amount of information about people if you know who to call, what to ask, and if you treat them well. "I send a lot of roses to secretaries," he said.

"Can you find out if he has any bank accounts?" I asked.

"No problem."

We shook hands and said goodbye. I drove back to campus, about a forty-five minute drive, and when I got to my desk, there was a message to call Mr. Boner.

"Do you have a pencil?" he asked. "Here is the address of his home and his office. He has no bank accounts yet."

The Vancouver tip had been the key to the discovery which made it a five minute job for Mr. Boner.

That was not the end of the story. A week or so later, there was another article in the Sunday paper. Mr. Boner had disappeared. Michigan Bell was particularly concerned because of the size of the unpaid phone bill he had left behind.

This was *Highway To Heaven* stuff. Mr. Boner--maybe he was a fictional character after all--was a guardian angel if ever there was one. He appeared at just the right moment for me and then he was gone. How can I not believe in miracles?

Armed with the information on Bob's whereabouts, I went to the Friend of the Court to activate collection procedures. They took the information, then informed me that there was nothing they could do because reciprocal agreements with Canada were on a state-to-province basis and Michigan did not have such an agreement with British Columbia. Another setback but I was determined to find a way.

One Sunday evening I came across a TV program on the Canadian channel called *Ombudsman*. I watched as they solved consumer problems and knew what I would do next. I wrote a letter detailing my problem and mailed it the next day.

Within a month I had a phone call from Toronto from Anne McCorquedale at the CBC. She told me that she had discovered that British Columbia and Michigan had signed a reciprocal agreement that had gone into effect on January first. She told me what legal papers to send and gave me the name of the person expecting them.

When I returned to the court and told them what I needed, they said they had no knowledge of such an agreement even though it had been in effect for three months!

"Here is the person's name and address," I said. "Why don't you call and verify it?"

"Policy does not allow us to make long distance calls," the agent said.

I secured all the papers and sent them myself. Eventually the Friend of the Court caught up with the process and sent duplicates but by then everything was in motion. The Canadian court verified the documents and ordered Bob to begin payments or go to prison. They even specified the address and cell number he would report to if he did not pay by May 31st. The checks were a quarter of what they should have been--coincidentally the same amount that Jerry had been giving me. I was so grateful for that much that I didn't question the amount until they stopped a few years later.

Then they discovered that the order had been misinterpreted. Again the Canadian courts came to the rescue, assigned me a lawyer, and ten years after Bob's departure we agreed to settle the arrearage for a tidy sum. By then the children were out of college and on their own but what a struggle it had been for all of us.

Thank heaven I had resolved my childhood traumas. Therapy had freed me to react to present calamities as an adult. Empowered with all the skills I had learned, I could finally ask for help as I never could as a child. I was on my own but I didn't have to be alone.

We're All In This Together

"Oh Lord, I'm tired of being poor. I want to be rich." I didn't think of it as a prayer at the time. It was more a cry of desperation.

Jerry and I had been married for eight months. He had spent two of those months either in the hospital or recovering from the effects of the tests and biopsies involved in the kidney problems he was having. His boss was getting impatient. Jerry's income depended on commissions from his sales, mine on part-time teaching and availability of classes. We started off with nothing and things were not getting better.

I was tired. I had been stretching every penny for more than a year--since Bob had left the country--measuring every portion, just making it through month by month. I said the fateful words after once more paying bills that left nothing in my checking account.

The Haven Hill lessons about the power of our desires were the farthest thing from my mind, but I would soon be reminded that there is a price to pay for the fulfillment of our desires. I learned the price of my prayer in very short order.

"I've lost my job." Jerry stood at the door late that afternoon looking dejected.

Lord, that's not exactly what I had in mind, I said to myself. For the next six months we scraped by on his remaining commissions, unemployment compensation, and a summer class that turned up unexpectedly. He also lost his company car so our only transportation was my little Gremlin which, on at least occasion, had to carry all six of us and Babe, our golden lab.

I felt poor in April but things got worse with no regular paycheck and no sign of a job in sight for either of us. My dissertation was not quite finished and my fellowship had run out. Fortunately rags and long hair were in--the hippie years–which saved us clothing and haircut allowances for the kids. They also earned their own spending money doing yard work, baby sitting and whatever came their way. Jerry and I celebrated our first anniversary with a steak dinner at Ponderosa--with a coupon.

In October, I sat on the edge of the bed crying while Jerry was getting dressed. "We have enough food to last for a week," I sobbed. "Then I don't know what we'll do. You have to find a job."

I opened the *Free Press* and started to read the want ads. The miracle began. There was an ad for an industrial battery salesman for Exide Corporation, the oldest company in the industry. Jerry had worked miracles as the sales manager for a local battery manufacturer where he had learned the business. He had established a good reputation. He called for an appointment and we sat down to strategize his approach. He had lost out on one opportunity for a similar position because they would not meet his price. It was time to lower our standards.

We calculated the minimum amount we needed to make his child support payments, house payments on our house, his ex-wife's house, the cottage, and basic living expenses. He asked for that.

He came home from his interview with the District Manager grumbling, "He said the salary was no problem. I should have asked for more."

He found out later that the salaries of the other salesmen had been raised to match his. We wouldn't get rich but we could live on it. That was the first step on our road to riches.

123

Three months later the stationary battery specialist at the office fell ill and could not attend a sales meeting scheduled in Hilton Head. Jerry went in his place. At that meeting a new product was introduced. Jerry recognized its potential immediately. It was the product of the future. He came back eager to present it to his customers. He became one of the first sales experts in the field of uninterruptible power supplies for computers. At that time computers were room sized and required controlled environments and power. The automotive companies in Michigan were his first customers.

A year later Exide spun off the UPS business to Exide Electronics and Jerry became the manufacturer's representative for the state. We had a lot to learn as we started our own business. It took another five years to really to pay off.

When we look back to those years, we don't know how we managed. We had barely enough money to survive, but our lives were rich with friends and family, the things that really count. I have always felt that my prayer set into motion the series of circumstances that led to our success. The wonder of it is that there were so many people involved in the venture, each with his or her own desires shaping circumstances.

At Haven Hill I had come to see the world as a network of people held together by the presence of God in each of us. Seeing the world in that way, I came to feel that I had planned my life before I arrived on this earth. I had chosen the circumstances I would live through and the people I needed to learn what I needed to know. As long as I made good choices as I proceeded through life, I would be safe and everything would work out well.

This shed new light on the premonitions I had often had and the recognition of familiar territory at various turning points in my life like the electric moment when I first met Bob in the classroom and felt I already knew him and the dark-of-night recognition of my doomed marriage. People had popped into my life when I needed them with that same familiarity: Jerry. And Ginny, who led me to

Haven Hill and others I have not mentioned. Sometimes they disappeared as quickly when our work was done as had Mr. Boner and his fast talk on the telephone.

I found some of them unattractive at first but my intuition propelled me to break through my resistance to them. There were lessons to learn if only to accept the darker parts of my psyche as I had with Hank. Nan was one of those, too. Alarm bells sounded at our first meeting but I needed her to release my childhood terror on that icy night at Haven Hill. Then there was brilliant Hal, who tended to push people away or at least keep them at a distance. He became a close friend and his help saved our business when our original partnership fell apart.

I see the people in my life held together in a mysterious force field. Woody's death was my first experience of this power. When his positive influence on the world was gone, it was not just the sense of loss we felt. It was more. Everything seemed to shift.

My mother had depended on him to stabilize her rebellious nature. He could always bring her back to rationality with a few words. Now she seemed almost frantic in her search for someone to take care of her. When I was unable to do it, she turned to her older sister in Florida and eventually made a new life for herself there.

Within a year of Woody's death, my marriage completely fell apart, but not just mine. Family friends we had known for over twenty-five years shocked us with a separation and divorce. He was an alcoholic and we had never suspected. We had all whirled around Woody, held in place by the force of his presence. When he was gone, we shot off in all directions.

I felt a similar release when my beloved Pastor Born died. He had been one of the most profound influences on my life after my arrival in Detroit at age eleven. Only once had I come close to leaving his church which I loved so dearly. When Bob and I moved to Dearborn Heights, it was time for Tim to begin Sunday School. We decided to join a church closer to home and to crown the move by having our soon-to-be-born baby baptized there. Laura was due within the month. When we spoke to Pastor Born about a transfer, he pleaded, "You'll let me baptize the baby, won't you?" I looked into his eyes and could not refuse. We scrapped our plans. I promised myself that as long as he was there, I would not leave Holy Cross.

Eventually we sent the children to school at Emmanuel in Dearborn but we maintained our membership at Holy Cross. Soon after that Bob stopped attending church with us. His path led him in other directions.

Pastor Born helped me through my two years of separation and my divorce. Three years later, he married Jerry and me and welcomed him to communion. When he became ill, services were often conducted by our assistant pastor. Pastor Born would preach occasionally but he was nearly blind, unable to walk without support, and had to be assisted into the pulpit by an attending usher. Still he was vibrant as always. Eventually he retired to California and we attended Emmanuel regularly but still did not transfer our membership. One Sunday Jerry and I decided it was time to speak to the pastor about joining the congregation and mentioned it to him as we left.

The next morning I read Pastor Born's death notice in the paper. I felt like I was in the twilight zone. My earthly connection to him had been broken and I had felt it four thousand miles away.

I paid my last visit to Pastor Born as he lay in state in front of the altar in the church that had been my home for thirty-five years. The click of my heels on the polished slate echoed in the empty church. The afternoon sun streamed through the stained glass, lighting the dust motes in the air.

I was flooded with memories of times I had walked down the aisle, first in the old church--now the school's gym--as a flag bearer one Fourth of July, in a new outfit every year for the children's Christmas program, in choir robes, my confirmation robe, then in this new Gothic church in my wedding gown, and with my babies in a

126

christening dress I had embroidered and stitched by hand.

A carved wooden cross soars above the altar, covered with dozens of lilies at Easter when Pastor Born's voice boomed into every corner of the packed church, "Christ is risen, hallelujah. He is risen indeed, hallelujah." I said goodbye to him and to Holy Cross at the coffin and felt a loss almost as great as I had when my father died.

Once I recognized the existence of these person-to-person connections in life, I could see them around me everywhere, people helping each other knowingly or unknowingly. I am amazed and delighted at how widespread the networks of people can be and how far-reaching across time and space we influence each other. If I had any doubts, the summer of 1978 set them to rest for once and all.

August ended with a bang. Literally. We were winding up a day at the lake with Jerry's family. The boat and dock were buttoned up; the laundry, gathered; the car, packed. It was only four-thirty but we were due in Lansing for a gathering at my brother's house at six. I was putting away the last of the dishes downstairs in the kitchen.

Suddenly Steve's buddy Dave burst through the front door yelling. The only word I heard was "accident." I dashed up the stairs in time to see the bathroom door slam behind Dave's back. I stood outside the door, dish towel in hand, and waited anxiously with the others to hear what had happened. Dave came out of the bathroom looking confused. He was in a state of shock. His glasses were broken so he could not see clearly. The back seam of his pants was split from top to bottom.

His story came out in gasps as Jerry grabbed keys and wallet and we ran for the car. Mark's car had hit a tree. My son Steve was driving. Two women had driven Dave to our place. But he couldn't remember where the accident had happened. And he couldn't see well enough to recognize which road it was. They all looked alike as country roads do. We guessed from what he said where he might have been and drove frantically down the various roads around the cottage until we arrived at the accident scene. The county sheriffs were cleaning up the area and directed us to follow after the ambulance which had already left for U of M hospital.

"The kids are OK," called one of the men.

If I had seen the car, I would not have believed him. My protective blindness kicked in. I did not see the car. I was only thinking of the kids. I clung to the sheriffs words as we raced to the hospital.

We found Steve moaning on a gurney in an ER cubicle. He was having difficulty breathing.

"Why me?" he mumbled. "Why me?" He closed his eyes and stopped breathing.

I panicked and called for a nurse. By the time she arrived he had shuddered and begun his labored breathing again. The nurse explained that he had a broken rib that was making breathing painful but that he was in no danger. His injuries were mostly facial. They were waiting for the plastic surgeon to arrive to repair a long jagged cut between his lower lip and his chin where his teeth had penetrated and broken off on the steering wheel.

It took the doctor a couple of hours to stitch Steve's chin. While he was in surgery we checked on the other kids and talked to the parents who had arrived by then. Three of the kids were shaken up and bruised but otherwise all right. Andrea, in the passenger seat, was the most seriously injured. She suffered a trauma to her back that kept her hospitalized for several days and in a brace for several months.

After surgery the doctor recommended that they keep Steve overnight. They were concerned that his lung had been punctured by the broken rib. They released him the next day when they determined that the puncture was a quick in and out that left no damage.

Steve told us the story of the accident as we drove home. He had been driving Mark's old Mustang because he knew the roads. As they drove down Hankerd Road, he said jokingly, "Watch out.

Around this bend a tree jumps out in front of us."

Andrea, playing along, quickly fastened her seat belt. It may have saved her life. Over the rise and around the curve, the worn tires lost their grip on the drizzle-slicked road and the tree did indeed jump out in front of them. They hit it. How's that for premonition?

The following Friday we took Steve back to the hospital to have his stitches removed, then drove to the junkyard where the Mustang sat forlornly in its final resting place. I was horrified. I could not imagine how six-foot Steve had climbed through the side window, crushed to a slit between the caved-in roof and the squashed front end. His double-jointedness must have helped. We saw two notches in the steering wheel where his front teeth had lodged–all that orthodontia gone to waste.

Later we found out that things were not as bad as they might have been. The tree they hit was dead and therefore not as solid as it would have been if it were alive. It broke on impact and fell on the roof of the car. If the tree had been alive and strong, the consequences would have been far worse. That tree had died after being hit by Tim's father-in-law a couple of years earlier.

The people involved in the accident were connected in other ways. The girl in the back seat was the daughter of our lake neighbor, who was Jerry's mom's art teacher in Royal Oak. We learned this in our get-acquainted meeting when they first moved in. Andrea was the step-daughter of a classmate of Jerry's, a girl he had dated in high school. We discovered this when we met her at their twenty-fifth class reunion the next year. The accident happened at the edge of the parking lot of a state park on Half Moon Lake. The first person on the scene was a life guard from the park. He helped get the kids out of the car and gave what first aid he could. When Steve moved into his new dorm at Michigan State the next month, he was greeted by the young man who had come to his rescue, his new resident advisor.

Even Mark fared better than he might have. He had only basic insurance on his old car, but because Steve was driving, our more liberal coverage applied and Mark collected market value of the car which was surprisingly high because the Mustang was a classic.

It is a great comfort to know that the universe is unfolding as it should. But my journey was not yet over. There were events in my life that I did not fully understand. There were illusions I had to give up before I would find the serenity to accept the things I could not change.

The Men In My Life

When Dr. J dismissed my dream of the little girls dancing in their ruffled dresses while the elevator ascended with the coalman, he said I did not know men. He was wrong. Here is what I knew.

The first man in my life was Ray, my father if you will, the man who abandoned my mother and me even as I was conceived. I don't know when he first saw me. Mother would have no contact with him whatsoever, so if he came to see me when I was a baby, she would not be there.

When I was about three, Mother would dress me up and stand me on the front porch to wait alone until he picked me up for a visit. She did not even wave goodbye when I set off with him. He would put me in the front seat of his black coupe--a Terraplane--where I would sit scared to death. He drove too fast. Too rough. Too jerky. I couldn't see out. The gear shift knob jiggled frighteningly near my legs. It was the first car I ever rode in. I didn't like it at all. He took me to his house to play with his two boys. I didn't like them either. One night they had milk toast for supper. I had never seen such a thing. The yellow butter made marble patterns on the warm milk soaking the bread. It tasted funny and it was mushy. I refused to eat it.

I don't know how many visits of this kind there were. Few I

131

suspect. It could not have been a very happy time for anyone.

One Sunday afternoon I was sitting on the front porch steps of our house, yelling back and forth to the girl across the street. We were too young to cross and play with each other.

"Where's your father?" she shouted.

"Where's my father?" I called to my mother in the house.

"He fell in a ditch," she called back unaware of what was going on.

"He fell in a ditch," I yelled to the little girl across the street.

My mother stormed through the door and yanked me into the house. I didn't know what I had done to deserve her wrath. From that day on I pictured my father at the bottom of a huge excavation, car and all.

One day--I was about seven--Aunt Rose called me into the living room and there was Ray sitting on a straight chair just inside the front door, about as far in as he was allowed. He was leaning forward, elbows on his knees, head in his hands in what I might now call quiet desperation. He had a package on his lap. He gave it to me and I opened it. It was a sleepyhead doll, floppy pink plush with a funny looking celluloid face, its eyes painted closed. Its zippered body was meant to hold pajamas but it wasn't really big enough. I think it was a goodbye present. I think he moved away after that.

I did not hear from him again until I moved to Detroit when I was eleven. He sent me a picture of himself in his Army uniform. I looked at the man in the photo with his tilted officer's cap as I would any stranger. He was sort of average–looking, neither handsome nor bad-looking. My memory says he had a mustache but that seems unlikely since he was in the army. I had no particular interest in this man called my father. Woody was my dad.

Ray wrote me a few letters which I did not answer. One day Mother ambushed me when I arrived home from school and said she had received a letter from Ray accusing her of not letting me write to him.

"Sit down right now, " she commanded, "and write to him. Tell him that you don't like to write letters." She stood over my shoulder as I wrote, then mailed the letter herself. That was the end of that. I did not hear from Ray again for 34 years.

The next significant man in my life was Uncle Jim, a mousy man, good-natured by day, a monster at night. He and Aunt Rose played an alcoholic's game. They would notch the labels on whiskey bottles to check up on each other. When one of them would sneak a drink, he or she would simply fill the bottle to the notch with water. It worked for a while.

One Halloween Aunt Rose dressed me for a school party as Alice in Wonderland, one of my favorite stories. I carried a bottle labeled, "Drink Me." Perhaps even then I wished for a magic potion that could make me small or tall. If whiskey could produce such monstrous results, why not my own elixir to keep me out of sight.

The third man in my life was my mother's younger brother. He and my Aunt Ann, my cousins Joanne and baby Richard, lived upstairs in the house on Grace. Uncle Steve was a red-headed, rowdy, iron-muscled bully with a nasty sense of humor, who loved to play practical jokes and laugh at other people's discomfort. When they were kids, he had thrown my mother out of a tree once and broken her arm. He was a fireman on the railroad when the job meant feeding the fire in the engine with shovels of coal.

Every summer I looked forward to the day when Uncle Steve took my cousins and me to Sandy Beach. It was an all day excursion complete with Aunt Ann's lavish picnic lunch. After the long drive Joanne and I would race across the hot sand, tearing off our clothes which we wore over our bathing suits. We would inch our way slowly into the sun-warmed shallows of Lake Erie with the foam of the gentle waves breaking over our feet, then our legs. We would squeal when it reached our bathing suits and push our way against the waves to deeper water, as far as we could until the water was up to our necks, shriek when the waves splashed our faces then race back to shore. I did not know how to swim but would pretend by resting on my arms on the bottom, letting my body float in the gentle waves lapping the shore.

All day we were in and out of the water. We would play at water's edge filling our pails with damp sand and plopping out cakes to bake in the sun. We would build sand castles that never turned out like the elaborate turrets and moats I pictured in my mind, but it didn't matter because my pesky little cousin Richard would knock them down anyway.

At lunchtime Aunt Ann would open the picnic basket and we would dive into fried chicken, potato salad, cookies, and lemonade. Everything tasted better at the beach on a blanket. No picnic tables for us.

It was an idyllic day except for one thing. At some moment when I least expected it, Uncle Steve would grab the top of my head in his iron grip and push me under the water. My fighting and flailing were useless. When my lungs were ready to burst, he would finally let go. I would come up gasping while he laughed and splashed more water in my face. My tears mingled with the water pouring down my face from my hair. It was the price I had to pay for my wonderful day at the beach.

I would eventually learn to swim well enough to pass the basic swimming test at summer camp so I could swim in the deeper, roped-off section of Clear Lake, but I was never comfortable in the water. As a teenager I cavorted in the lake with friends, swimming to the raft in near panic until I reached the ladder and climbed up.

When my children were babies, I took them to the community pool and taught them to enjoy the water in the safety of my arms, to kick their legs at the side of the pool, to float with a steadying hand under their backs. They were strong swimmers by the time they went to school and I retired to a deck chair, not admitting my fear of the water until I looked back at my childhood through adult eyes.

I spent a lot of time with my cousins, in the house on Grace until I was six or seven, then in their house when they moved to the country where I often spent weekends with them. I loved their new brick house, two stories, a breakfast nook, a shower, and Joanne had her own room. I thought they were rich. Joanne and I loved to water the vegetable garden in the backyard where we sometimes picked peas and beans. They had a beautiful yard and a creeping bent lawn that we were not allowed to set foot on, Uncle Steve's pride and joy.

Aunt Ann made us chocolate pancakes for breakfast. She made my favorite Slovak dishes that Gramma used to make, especially *bobalki*, a concoction of sweet yeast bread soaked in milk, honey and poppy seeds, best served warm. She took us berry picking in the fields and made jam from the wild raspberries and strawberries that we brought home. We picked arm loads of tiger lilies from the roadsides.

We liked to sit on the couch in their sunny living room and sing hymns from the hymn book. We looked at old-fashioned pictures in the stereopticon. Aunt Ann let Joanne and me wash dishes standing on a stool, wrapped in big aprons, at the sink overflowing with suds. Joanne and I fought over who would wash while the other dried. I usually won. We played dress-up with a drawer full of Aunt Ann's old dresses, shoes, and purses. My favorite dress was a sheer dotted swiss, that marvelous blue the widow wore, with a full twirly skirt.

There was a brand new drive-in movie theater--the first one in town--across the field from their house. Joanne and I watched the shadowy pictures from the window of her bedroom when we were supposed to be sleeping.

Jackie was born after they moved to the country. By then Joanne and I were old enough to take him for walks in his buggy and play house with our real live baby. Unlike rough-and-tumble Richard--I hid my toys when they came to visit on Grace--Jackie was a quiet boy.

135

I loved the sunshine and the freedom of Aunt Ann's house. Until Uncle Steve came home. Then I grew small and hid within myself as invisible as I could be. I think the whole household did that, but it was my aunt people said was crazy.

It would be decades before I would piece together the whispers I heard as a child. At the time I thought Joanne was kind of dumb but she was younger and I thought that explained it. Aunt Hazel called her a nervous child. I heard the giggles about the enema bag lodged in the backyard tree. I knew Uncle Steve had pitched it out the window in a fit of rage. I didn't know why. I didn't know what it was used for. I was told to stay away from the man next door who was known to molest children, whatever that meant, but nothing was done about him. Secrets were whispered; that was the end of it.

The story of Sybil and her multiple personalities opened my eyes and the eyes of the world to the torture of the enema and the effects of early abuse and I began to understand.

Eventually Aunt Ann was diagnosed schizophrenic. By then Uncle Steve had divorced her. I lost contact with my grown-up cousins after the divorce. They remained loyal to their mother and would have nothing to do with their father's side of the family. I think of them with the same sadness I felt when I left behind the joy-filled days I spent with them when Uncle Steve was not around.

As a child I did not understand all this. I did not have words to conceptualize my fears but my unconscious gave me the vivid image of the coalman. The dream combined the gritty coalbin and the monster furnace in the basement where Mary Ann and I played, with Uncle Jim, who disturbed my sleep with his drunken ranting, and Uncle Steve, the railroad fireman who destroyed the joy of a happy household. Who says I didn't know men?

Where Was Your Mother?

I was fifty-six years old when I began to rid myself of the illusions I had about my mother. One of the final tasks in life is to look at our past with mature eyes and accept the reality that we find there. That phase began with Mother's Christmas visit in 1988.

I arrived at Detroit Metropolitan airport three weeks before Christmas to find that Mother's plane from Florida had arrived early, a rare occurrence especially at that time of year. I rushed to the gate and there was Mother sitting huddled in her winter coat, barricaded by the carry-on at her feet, her purse and a shopping bag in her lap. Mother has a way of protecting herself from the intimacy of hello hugs.

Apparently the physical barrier was not enough. "I like your hair short," she said without so much as a hello. I had let my hair grow into a medium bob, admittedly not my most flattering hairdo but a change from the short styles I have worn most of my life. This was a bad beginning to a visit that only got worse.

The ride home began with the usual complaints about airplane food or lack of, noisy children, tiring plane changes, etc. This was followed by her updates on her friends. Mother usually painted a very negative picture of her life in Florida that belied her assertions that she loved it and would never move north again. I never knew

137

which version to believe so I did not take her complaints seriously. I decided they were a smokescreen to conceal her satisfaction with her life from me. I tuned them out. In comparing notes with my brother who kept her for the second half of her month-long visit, I found that she saved her complaints for me. She told him everything was wine and roses or at least that's what he heard.

Mother and I quickly fell into the patterns of all our visits. The china tea cup, sugar bowl and creamer took up residence on the kitchen counter. Mother hated to drink from the mugs that were my preference. Water was heated in the kettle instead of the microwave and there was the endless grumbling about which switch turned on which burner when she made herself a cup, carefully saving the tea bag which I would have thrown away.

She protested when I waited on her but I sensed that she really expected it. Mother has a difficult time with thank yous. I watch for the way her eyes light up inadvertently when I take her by surprise with a treat like a poppy seed roll, a favorite Christmas treat, or bakery doughnuts, which they just don't know how to make in Vero Beach.

Over teacups the endless recital and repetition of her every-day life begins. Her only acknowledgment of our lives are the stock questions, "How is . . .?" Fill in the blank with one of the children's names or perhaps a friend or neighbor she still remembers. She never asks about me and I volunteer very little. She does not remember much of what I tell her anyway. I felt guilty about my feelings for my Mother. My parochial education had ingrained the fourth com-mandment into my being and I was able to honor her by responding to her needs but my treatment of her was hardly loving. I would start off with the best of intentions but was never able to sustain them.

One morning I decided to make a particular effort at con-versation. We had watched a Helen Hayes TV Christmas movie the night before and she had gone to bed, too tired to watch the end of it. As I made her toast and poured her coffee, I started to tell her the rest

138

of the story but she interrupted me after a sentence or so with an unrelated comment. It was as if she had not heard a word of what I said and did not care to. I sat down at the table with her and opened the newspaper.

During her second week with us, she made an appointment to have her hair done at Penney's in Fairlane Mall. I arranged for us to meet my daughter Laura for lunch afterward. I dropped Mother off for her appointment at eleven and told her I would return for her at twelve, then parked the car near Lord and Taylor where we would be lunching to save her a walk through the mall after lunch. I went off to finish my Christmas shopping, specifically a gift for Mother. Our family draws names and we each exchange one generous gift during the family celebration. We would be gathering at Laura's that year, but I wanted Mother to have a package to open with just us on Christmas morning. I bought her a soft pale green sweater and a pastel flowered blouse. I was feeling very pleased with my purchases as I soaked up the hustle and bustle of the mall on the way back to Penney's. Christmas can't be too commercial for me.

When I arrived at the salon Mother was not ready yet so I sat down in the waiting area next to a display case of cosmetics across from the reception desk. Eventually Mother came out with her hairdresser to settle her bill. The woman asked if someone was meeting her. She hissed, "My daughter. She can wait."

Her tone of voice bowled me over with its bitterness. She turned when she finished her transaction. I got to my feet and in as light a tone as I could muster, said, "Oh I can wait, can I?"

She looked up in surprise and without a blink brushed her hand at me and said coyly, "I saw you there."

"Did you?" I responded. Of course she hadn't. I was hidden from her view next to the display case directly behind her.

I helped her into her coat and we walked through the mall in silence. I was a bundle of mixed emotions: hurt, anger, and helplessness, but mostly amazement at the quick change from acidity to sweetness and the recognition of the depth of my mother's disdain for me which I had never acknowledged.

Fortunately Laura was her usual ebullient self at lunch and carried most of the conversational ball with little help from me. I had a lot to digest besides lunch.

On Christmas morning, when Mother opened her box, her eyes lit up. I knew I had chosen well. A few days later she returned the gift. The sweater was the new butt length and looked darling on her tiny figure. But she wore only her navy, gray, or brown polyester skirts and plain shirtwaist blouses with the classic acrylic cardigans of the early seventies.

After the beauty shop incident memories took on new meanings. The sound of her words echoes clearly even now. That exchange lifted a load of guilt from my shoulders. I was ashamed of my impatience, my inability to share my life with her, my lack of attention to her complaints. At last I realized that there was nothing I could do that would please her and it was no longer important to try.

Soon after that visit, I found myself in tears while reading Nancy Mairs' touching memoir, *Remembering the Bone House*, in which she describes her experience taking part in her mother's second wedding. I realized for the first time that I had not been included in the celebration when my mother married Woody. I cried deep wrenching sobs of abandonment that I had not dared feel as a child.

I cannot imagine not including my children in my wedding. Laura helped pick out my wedding dress and Tim gave me away. They sneaked champagne in collusion with my new brother-in-law at our reception. What kind of mother would not include her children on such a happy occasion? Why had it taken all those years--more than fifty--to realize that my mother was not the mother who really loved me and cared for me while she worked hard to provide us a living?

There were so many celebrations we did not share. She did not come to my senior play which I had a part in nor to the community theater productions I played in with one exception. I had the lead in *Mother Is a Freshman* and she came to see it but she brought my four-year-old brother and left during the first act when he started acting up.

She did not come to my college graduation but surprised me by coming unannounced from Lansing to Detroit with Woody for a very short and unceremonious initiation into Phi Beta Kappa. The ceremony, if you could call it that, took place in a crowded classroom and couldn't have lasted more that fifteen minutes. The celebration was a dinner that night. Had I known they wanted to come, I would have made reservations for them, but I didn't. I suspect they came because Woody wanted to show his pride in my achievement as best he could.

Mother did come to my first wedding--not my second--but I had made all the arrangements myself with the help of my friends. Her only contribution was to complain about the bad job the women of the church had done carving the turkey, a complaint she ultimately voiced to the woman in charge. I was embarrassed for years every time I saw the woman in church.

Mother and I did have some good years, especially after I was married and when I had my babies. I think my years as a housewife and mother recalled her best years when she left her job to keep house and be a mother when my brother was born. She often babysat on weekends when Bob and I traveled, staying at our house or keeping the kids at hers in Lansing. During those years she would come to Detroit for visits and we would shop and go to lunch like girl friends. She could relate to me as a housewife and mother, but not to my other accomplishments.

After Woody's death Mother turned to me to fill the emotional vacuum of her widowhood. I brought her home with us after the funeral because I didn't want her to spend the holidays alone. I welcomed her into our household but probably should not have. It encouraged her emotional dependence. Mother never truly lived in

141

her house again. She went back a few times-- usually with a friend--to dispose of Woody's things and do what was necessary to sell the house but that year she lived a transient life, spending a month or so with her sister in Florida, staying with us either at home or, when the weather warmed, at the cottage. I think she wanted me to invite her to live with us permanently.

She began looking for an apartment in spring, not in Lansing where her friends and my brother lived, but in our area, to be near our family. I drove her to various complexes nearby where there were lovely apartments available. None would do. Finally she added her name to the waiting list for an opening in the apartments neighboring our community, two blocks from our house. I should have objected but I was still in my powerless mode when it came to Mother. I had not yet discovered Melba and Haven Hill. She moved into her apartment in September and lived there for a year but never even hung a picture.

Our real trouble started after my separation. My divorce stirred all her unresolved feelings about her divorce. That's why she had pleaded with me not to get a divorce the day after that traumatic Thanksgiving dinner when everything fell apart. I couldn't deal with that nor with the clinging dependence that followed, nor with the constant complaining that grated on my ears.

One evening she came over to babysit while I went to the theater with Melba. We stopped at The Snug afterwards for hot chocolate--not even a bar--and when I returned after midnight, Mother was in a panic yelling about how worried she was about my being downtown alone at that hour. I told her that if she was going to be so upset, it was better that she not sit again. She agreed.

Sundays turned out to be a major problem. She wanted me to pick her up and take her to church with us. I desperately needed the spiritual nourishment Sunday services gave me at that time. The silence and presence of God were a respite from the hubbub of everyday life. Mother disrupted that with her complaints and criticisms. I could not tolerate her negativity. I reminded myself of the years when I went to church alone as a child taking the streetcar or the bus. I remembered when Woody started to go with me and Mother did not join us. I remembered that he later took my brother to Sunday School while Mother stayed home. It helped with some of my guilt.

I talked these things out with Melba and she helped me to realize that we would both be better off if I did not let her lean on me. She was only 60, young enough to begin a new life. She wanted to mingle her life with ours but this could not be and I knew it.

Finally she moved to Florida, bought a house near her sister and continued her restless life. She lived in her first house for a year then sold it. She made plans to move in with a friend, the woman she had worked for when I was a baby. But her friend died suddenly before the move and Mother, high and dry again, bought another house. She remarried and later regretted it. When her husband died, she sold her house and bought a condo. After her sister and her brother died, she moved north again, this time near my brother in Lansing.

At a meeting of my writers' group, after reading a part of my early life, a friend asked in an astounded tone, "Where was your mother?"

Where was she indeed? She had seen that my basic needs were supplied and I am grateful for that. The true gifts she gave me were Aunt Hazel and Woody who gave me the love and respect that she could not give me herself and I am truly grateful for that. It is not easy to realize that your mother did not--and does not--love you. I do know that she wanted to. We all want loving mothers. Still it was a relief to know it. While I am sad that Mother will never really know me, I have accepted what I cannot change with some serenity.

That serenity was shaken at lunch with Laura one day. When the conversation turned to my relationship with Mother, I told her that I had accepted the fact that Mother and I would never resolve our differences.

"Mom," she said, "Gramma has told me things that she says I shouldn't tell you. I don't know whether to tell you now or wait til she dies."

"Now," I said without hesitation. "It's the only way for any hope of healing."

I could see Laura's inner struggle to find the words. "She says that whenever she sees you, it brings back the awful memories of what happened when you were born I don't think she ever got over your father's betrayal. That's why she can't stand to be with you."

My heart broke as I watched the pain in Laura's eyes as she said this. Laura loved us both. It was her dearest hope that Mother and I would have a joy-filled reconciliation.

"I know that, Laura," I reassured her. "I've known that for a long time."

"And she's jealous of you," she blurted.

"I know that too. I watched a talk show one day about mothers who are jealous of their daughters and I recognized Gramma and me. But I don't understand why."

"I think it's because you're so smart and do things she could never do."

If we hadn't been across from each other in a restaurant booth, I would have hugged her. As it was, all I could do was thank her for telling me. "It helps a lot to know that what I thought was so really is so. I'm glad you don't have to carry the burden of that secret by yourself anymore."

I was furious at Mother for laying on my beautiful daughter her own dark secrets and demanding that she keep them to herself. I thought back to the day when Laura called me from her car on her return from a visit with her grandmother. She was on the verge of tears as she recounted her grandmother's words and the scathing tone of her voice, "What does your mother do in the office anyhow?"

She was referring to Jerry's and my manufacturer's rep agency where Laura was a very successful sales engineer selling electronic equipment. "I told her you do all the detail work, the accounting, and the computer work. I told her we I didn't know what we would do without you."

"Mom, she doesn't even know you." I could tell she was crying. "I don't want that to happen to us," she said desperately.

"It won't, Laura. We are going to continue talking to each other about the important things in our lives."

I thought of her driving the expressway in her distressed state and did my best to reassure her. "Mother has never really approved of me. You and I both appreciate each other and when something goes wrong, we talk about it. We'll be fine."

Most of all I did not want to sour her good relationship with my mother which gives them both pleasure. I hated seeing her split by the two most important women in her life. I hope that she has now come to the same sad acceptance I have that Mother will never know me and I am all right with it but all the more determined that the same thing will not happen to Laura and me. Some family traditions should not be passed on.

Unfortunately a few years later, when Jerry and I had retired and Laura took over the business, our relationship became strained. We appreciate each other but rarely talk about important things except for occasional business matters. We see each other at family gatherings and at rare lunches or dinners when conversations are superficial. Now that we live in Arizona we do not see her at all. I miss my daughter. But I'm thankful for the internet.

Mother, Mother

Mother wrote this penultimate chapter of my story. I had finished the last chapter when my brother called me one Friday afternoon to say that Mother was in intensive care at Sparrow Hospital. She had been taken to emergency vomiting massive amounts of blood.

As Jerry and I drove the hour and a half to Lansing, I pondered on how Mother's death would affect me. I had done my grieving for her when I had given up my illusions of her being a loving mother. Still there was the niggling thought that some old guilt or longing would engulf me when she was gone.

When I saw her lying helplessly in bed hooked up to an IV, a naso-gastric tube taped to her nose, a catheter draining cloudy fluid from her bladder, my heart went out to her. I saw a hero, who had lived an odyssey of her own. No matter that many of her problems were of her own making. She had suffered and survived and was suffering again. I knew her dying would not be easy. I knew I would help her as best I could.

Remarkably she looked better than I expected her to: good color, alert, but very tired. She actually flirted with the gastro-enterologist who said that he would scope her stomach--the source of the bleeding--the next day. He thought the episode was brought

146

on by a combination of her arthritis medication and a drug she had taken for a bladder infection. Jerry and I stayed with her that afternoon along with my brother Rob. Later his wife Renie and their daughter Melissa came in. When Mother was settled for the night, we all went out to dinner at Clara's, the converted Lansing train station. Our mood was almost festive as we feasted variously on nachos, chicken enchiladas and pasta, and assured each other that Mother was in good hands.

On the drive home Jerry and I talked and laughed. We had said once that Mother would live til her money ran out, then leave us. It looked like this might be the case. We agreed that Mother would not go gently into that good night. She would die as she had lived, kicking and screaming. I was grateful for my own peace of mind. The next morning I received another call from my very distraught brother. Mother had taken a turn for the worse. He had been called to the hospital at 3:30 A.M. to discuss treatment options. Mother's living will specified no heroic measures and this would be honored. Treatment would be conservative. The scope was postponed. Her comfort was the primary concern. They did give her blood.

I called my kids and suggested that it would be a good day to visit while she was still alert. When I talked to Laura later that day, it appeared they had all had a lot of fun together, reminiscing and cracking jokes with her. It sounded like a party in ICU. That night they moved her to a standard ward where she promptly tore out the naso-gastric tube. They decided to leave it out. Sunday passed without incident except for her complaints: we had left her with a bunch of strangers.

On Monday Rob called with the news that she had had a major heart attack and had been moved to cardiac care. The cardiologist told Rob that she had valve damage which would be fatal without surgery. They reported this to Mother and she responded, "I'm 88 [actually 85] years old. I don't want surgery."

147

When I saw her again on Tuesday, still in ICU, she was wired to numerous machines monitoring oxygen levels, blood pressure, heartbeat, and IV intake. Her hands and arms were black and blue from needles where they had punctured her for blood samples and the insertion of wires and tubes. A naso-gastric tube was again taped to her nose, this time covered by an oxygen mask. She could barely respond to us and asked only for ice chips to quench her thirst. Weak and uncomfortable, she spent the day in a haze of morphine.

"Don't leave me alone," she pleaded. We didn't. We took turns at her bedside, at times simply holding her hand.

That afternoon I watched in horror as a med tech struggled to take blood for a test causing further bruising and swelling to her already mutilated hand. Even the tech was upset. After that Rob and I talked to her nurse and we agreed: no more tests, cut the drugs supporting her heart and blood pressure. Let her go. Rob would talk to the doctor in the morning.

Mysteriously Mother's hands and feet were hot and we repeatedly wrapped them in damp cloths and massaged her feet with lotion to cool them. With a malfunctioning heart valve, we expected cold extremities because of restricted circulation. The doctor had no explanation for this.

At 8:00 P.M. my brother tucked her in with a blessing. Again we went to dinner. This time we compared family stories and filled in the blanks in each other's memories. We had begun the mourning process.

The next two days--without the drugs--were good days. She was alert and reasonably comfortable.

"Just like Mother," I said to Jerry, "she puts on her party face for everyone else and saves her pain for me."

He laughed. "Why should she change now?"

On Friday we returned to spend the weekend and take our turns at her bedside. She was even worse, this time moaning, "I give up. I can't take it."

Her blood pressure and pulse were not alarmingly low. Her heart, while somewhat irregular, was pumping along doing its job as best it could. Mother was not about to leave without a struggle. I prayed for easy passage.

The doctor examined her and said she had fluid in her lungs, an expected effect of the heart malfunction. "She will die without surgery," he said, "but I agree with your decision. Her chances of surviving the table are only ten per cent."

He then suggested tube feeding. "Why?" I asked.

"Why not?" he replied. "We don't like to starve our patients."

I looked at Mother weakly clinging to life, then back at this man who would prolong her agony. "I know you're not God," I said, "but can you give us some idea of time? Are we talking weeks? Days?"

"Days," he replied. " The only reason she is living is because she is resting and putting no strain on her heart. If she were up and moving, her heart would give out."

"Then I see no point in tube feeding."

He agreed to wait a few days. I asked if she might be able to tolerate jello or custard. I thought it might taste good and feel good in her dry mouth. He agreed to try it.

With no treatment measures in place, we knew the hospital would not keep her for long. It was time to talk hospice. We called in the social worker to consider our alternatives. She gave us a list of nursing homes with hospice beds available and suggested that we look them over. She said she would meet with us on Monday to make arrangements.

That night they moved Mother back to a semi-private room, free of all wires except the IV and oxygen. Again she pulled out the naso-gastric tube. In the morning she was confused and incoherent. The doctor said it was the first sign of the brain shutting down to ease the dying process. We could expect longer periods of sleep and eventually a deep coma.

Now her hands and feet were cold and we rubbed them to warm them. She was in and out of consciousness, taking morphine for comfort, and we thought the end was near. Perhaps she would die before we had to move her again.

On Sunday she was alert again and warm. Her bruises were healing. "When can I go back to my apartment?" she asked.

The doctor said the fluid in her lungs was receding. I asked if we should reevaluate our plans and he shook his head no.

That afternoon while Laura was there, Mother applauded when Kurt Gibson hit a home run during the Tiger game her roommate was watching. That night all hell broke loose.

I had been living in expectation of Rob's calls and shuddered every time the phone rang. I did not expect to hear what he said on Monday morning.

"You'd better sit down," he began. "Last night Mom pulled off the oxygen mask, tore out the catheter, climbed over the rails on her bed and sat on the portable commode--her roommate's--next to her bed, scared the poor woman out of her skin. This morning she told off the doctor."

The doctor, a newly assigned resident, explained that he had not seen her before. "You doctors are all alike,"she said. "All you're interested in is your money and your diamonds. Well you can take your diamonds and shove them up your ass."

Her roommate cheered her on, "Go, Helen," and her visiting husband laughed and added, "Yeah, yeah."

"She was furious at me," my brother went on. "She held up her arms and said, 'Look at this. You've had me nailed down in this place for a week. I don't want you here. The only person I want to see is Renie.'"

I was roaring with laughter as he dramatically recounted the events of the night and the morning to me and then repeated the story to Laura.

"That's Mother," I said.

150

"It runs in the family," said Laura.

On Saturday Rob and I had looked at hospices and chosen burial clothes. We sat in Mother's apartment and talked about the disposition of her furniture and when we would move it out. Now we talked about what arrangements we would make to move her back there. It would kill her to be put in a nursing home.

When the ulcer revealed by the stomach scope had healed, she was able to eat a normal diet. With daily physical therapy she was able to walk again and was getting her strength back. Eleven days later she returned to her apartment spurning the walker they had given her for her recuperation and lived an active life for five more years.

Amazing Grace

"Amazing grace, how sweet the word." My throat swelled and tears came to my eyes when I first heard the plaintive voice of Judy Collins sing those words at a sensitivity session where a group of us had gathered between semesters .

The old hymn became a hit record of the late sixties because of Judy's touching rendition. It became the theme song at Haven Hill. We sang it during our improvised services on Sunday mornings and sometimes at singalongs after evening sessions. When I hear the hymn, I think of cozy evenings of shared feelings and of the morning sun streaming through the stained glass behind the altar at St. Basil's where Haven Hill ongoers continued to meet after the yearly seminar was discontinued. The hymn is the theme of my life.

I look back with wonder at the grace that has guided me, protected me, and showered me with blessings. I was born on a street named Grace. I have walked in grace all my life, even in my darkest days. Woody said it in his characteristically colorful language: "You could fall in a barrel of shit and come out smelling like a rose."

I didn't know it was so obvious, but Jerry noticed it too. He is an excellent driver but often drives very close to the edge. When I get nervous, he laughs and says that as long as I am in the car, he is safe. I prefer not to test it.

I know that my needs are well provided for even in small ways. One day at noon I was making my run from my eleven o'clock class at Detroit College of Business to my one o'clock class at Henry Ford Community College. I had one hour to make the ten minute drive, gobble down a sandwich and get my stuff together. That day I had a flat tire as I turned onto Ford Road. I pulled into a parking lot and two scruffy young boys–they couldn't have been older than ten–came running up to help. They changed the tire under my supervision--a skill learned from a recent student's demonstration speech--and I was on my way on time for class. Guardian angels come in all shapes and sizes.

I am not good at remembering jokes but I do remember the story of the approaching flood when an old couple was warned to leave their home because of the rising waters. "No," they said, "God will save us." As the waters rose, they climbed out onto their roof where a man in a rowboat approached and shouted for them to climb in. "No," they said, "God will save us. "As conditions worsened, a helicopter hovered overhead and dropped a rope ladder. "No," they said, "God will save us." Of course the couple drowned. When they reached the pearly gates, they asked St. Peter why God had abandoned them.

"He warned you about the flood," said St. Peter. "Then he sent a boat. He even sent a helicopter. That was about all He could do."

Grace surrounds us, if we only recognize it. It is often disguised. It prods us from within, sometimes as conscience, sometimes as intuition. All it requires is that we be alert to it, to pay attention.

When I heard about Wayne State's Graduate Fellowship, I did not apply for it because it was not enough money to support the kids and me and the fellowship prohibited teaching during the year of the grant so I would not be able to supplement my income if I got it. A couple of months later I walked into the mail room to check my box and noticed the Fellowship brochures on the counter. Idly I picked

153

one up and took it to my office to read. It was late Thursday afternoon. The deadline was the next day.

This time as I read, I realized that it would pay extra money for dependents. I had four. It would also pay for my dissertation hours. Those two things doubled the dollar value of the Fellowship. But did I have time to put together all the information I needed to turn in? I called the Graduate Office and asked what the last possible moment was that I could turn in the material. The secretary said the files would be turned over to the committee at noon on Tuesday. If I got my forms there by that time, they would be included.

I called Dr. Bohman, the chairman of the department, and explained what I was doing. "Can you write a letter of recommendation for me for the fellowship?"

"Of course, I will," he said. "I will come in tomorrow and write it for you." He did not usually come in on Fridays. I knew that he truly cared about his students but it seemed extraordinary for him to make such an offer.

"No," I said. "I talked to the Graduate Office and they said I can have until Tuesday noon."

"I will have the letter for you Monday then."

I spent the next day and the weekend arranging for transcripts, putting together my vita, writing my plan for the future, and my philosophy of education, all required for the application. By Tuesday everything was in order and I delivered it to the Graduate Office with many thanks to the secretary who had extended the time limit for me.

I ultimately received the Fellowship and it saved us during the tumultuous year when I remarried and Jerry lost his job.

What was it that made that brochure pop up in front of me that day in the mail room? It had been there all along. It was the rowboat that I turned down. Thank goodness I recognized the helicopter even without the thunking of its rotors.

Grace is what I feel when I say that I planned my life before I was born and chose the people who would help me along the way.

As a child, grace protected me from the abuse and the craziness that surrounded me when my grandmother left. Grace brought Aunt Hazel and Woody and Pastor Born into my life during those critical growing up years. At the right moment it brought me Melba, at the prime of her counseling career--she later suffered a stroke and never practiced in the same way again--then Haven Hill, discontinued after my last session when the lodge was closed to weekend conferences and eventually to all meetings. Later it was vandalized, burned, and torn down. I wanted to revisit it as I wrote this but it was gone and I had to rely on my memories.

Grace has given me all good things in life and the strength to deal with all the tough stuff. I think of it as the circle of light that haloed my grandmother reading the Bible at my bedside, the light that lit my way to my attic refuge at Aunt Hazel's, the white light that protects us when danger threatens and leads us on when we approach death.

I was born in grace and my grandmother took me into her arms. I shall die in grace and I know that my grandmother's arms will welcome me into eternity.

Gerry Tamm received her PhD in Communication, Rhetoric and Public Address from Wayne State University in 1976. She has taught in various colleges and senior programs, applied her skill in the business world, and pursued her interest in writing and publishing poetry as well as prose. Her previous memoirs are *Making Sense: An Elder's Task* and *Choosing Life: A Diary of Grace.* She lives in a retirement community in Tucson, Arizona.

Made in the USA
San Bernardino, CA
24 June 2017